Amberley Church:
A Critical Appreciation

AMBERLEY CHURCH

A Critical Appreciation

NIGEL FOXELL

MENARD PRESS

Amberley Church; A Critical Appreciation
© 2005 Nigel Foxell

ISBN 1 874320 54 3

Menard Press
8 The Oaks, Woodside Avenue, London N12 8AR, UK
Tel. + 44 (0) 8446 5571   Fax + 44 (0) 8445 2990
Email: Rudolf@Menardpress.co.uk
www.Menardpress.co.uk

Worldwide Distribution and Representation
(except North America)
Inpress Limited, Northumberland House
11 The Pavement, Popes Lane, Ealing, London W5 4NG
Tel: 020 8832 7464   Fax: 020 8832 7465
Email: stephanie@inpressbooks.co.uk
www.Inpressbooks.co.uk

Distribution in North America
Small Press Distribution Inc.
1341 Seventh Street, Berkeley, CA 94710, USA
www.spdbooks.org

Typeset by Antony Gray
Printed in Great Britain by
Cambridge University Press

*To those who ensure that
St Michael's Church, Amberley,
is open all day, every day.*

Contents

'We went to Amberley yesterday . . . an astonishing forgotten lovely place, between watermeadows and downs.'

VIRGINIA WOOLF

'I have always found when I have been there that the principal inhabitants of the village (apart from artists) are cows ambling peacefully between the cottages, udders swinging, tails swishing, brown eyes gazing at nothing in particular, attended by remarkably small boys kicking up the white dust.'

ESTHER MEYNELL

' . . . little, lost Down churches praise
The Lord who made the hills.'

RUDYARD KIPLING

Amberley Church in Brief

Amberley almost certainly had an Anglo-Saxon church, but the one that we know was founded c.1103. Since then, every century from the twelfth to the twenty-first has left signs, chief of which are the extension to the original chancel in 1230, and, at no very different date, the south aisle and the tower. This is a way of saying that what began as pure Romanesque was enlarged during the early stage of – yes – Gothic, the first new style since classical times.

From the Middle Ages there are murals and a monumental brass, and inscriptions that stretch from the first half of the eighteenth century to the second half of the twentieth. Mostly, however, the furnishings and decorative elements date from the first third of the twentieth century. The earliest of these are Neo-gothic, while the latest show signs of Modernism, which was the first new style since Gothic.

The Setting

'Sussex by the sea,' wrote Rudyard Kipling, and sure enough this long, slender county is a Channel-hugging one. But our Amberley, twelve kilometres from pebbly Clymping beach, has no seascape to offer, only landscape. It has *two* landscapes in fact: the Weald to the north, and, to the south, the Downs, a chain of hills that on dark nights become the bison of Burpham.

These Downs separate the village from the coastal plain. And no mistake! On the other hand you need only climb their nearest point – 'Amberley Mount', we call it, or simply 'The Mount' – to catch a glimpse of Littlehampton, and imagine France. To the south-west of us, moreover, is the Arun Gap, by which the Downs are themselves divided. 'Arun', a back-formation from 'Arundel', is a modern name for the River Tarrant. The tide reaches as high as Amberley, telling us that the mouth cannot be all that far; but with a six-hour delay.

Six hours. Quite a thought. But not one to deter your resourceful smuggler. On December 8th, 1804, *The Ipswich Journal* reported: 'Wednesday sennight during Divine Service some custom house officers entered the Parish Church at Amberley, in Sussex, and seized 18 tubs of contraband spirit which they found concealed in that sacred deposit.' And Alfred Noyes' Sussex tar, on finding himself in San Diego, sings of Amberley. Oh, of other spots, too; but of Amberley first, and not for alphabetical reasons, you may be sure.

On the evening of July 7th, 1839, a storm left no conservatory undamaged, but hailstones, not the sea, were to blame: some of them were nine inches in circumference. But I remember a day when sea was indeed what our normally placid wetlands looked like: waves broke on the western bank of Brook Road; and one farmer, a second Noah, gave houseroom to such animals as he could find, while water rose between his floorboards. And still we heard isolated moos, isolated indeed, human-sounding, yet other-worldly, like the cries of the wounded in no-man's-land.

Nearer to home, John Hatt of The Turnpike, just this side of Houghton Bridge, had to be rehoused. Even the curtain wall of the castle got its feet wet: a little notice tells you to what level. It tells you also when: November 6th–7th, 2000. But mercifully the village itself is perched high enough to escape drowning – though springs threaten.

*   *   *

The Setting

At this moment, as I write, a seed-hopper, ascending and descending the lowest slope of the Downs, is pursued by a wake of gulls. They bring the smell of the sea with them. But we who live here (or partly live) are landlubbers unabashed, tucked away in what Dickens called 'the inland green'. And happily enough. If you believe Walton, 'Amerley trout' is one of the four good things of Sussex; nor need you question whether he meant the freshwater variety.

It follows that beach pebbles – they help clad the coastal town – are not our style. True, they have colonized one waist-high wall in Church Street, but they are grey, those oval faces – from homesickness.

*   *   *

At Church Street's far end is the churchyard, and I suppose you will tell me that that, at least, has a salt air. Those headstones! How they lean! Sail in a gale! But the thick-walled church says 'land', terra firma. Cryptless, on upper greensand rock, it is something of a rock itself.

As is the castle. And its battlements look soilwards, a ward against rebellious peasants, not marauding French sailors. For downstream, mercifully, sat the Earl of Arundel. Of Arundel? Nay, of Arundel Castle, which was a second Windsor, and match for anyone.

The summer of 1940 presented a different threat. And what would Sea-lion have discovered? That Amberley had its very own pillbox. But it commanded the railroad, not the river or its estuary. And if the lion had come from the sky?

13

Michael, Patron Saint of Amberley

The parish magazine for August, 1898, contains this entry: 'In other places where the Church is dedicated to St Michael, it is found to be a good plan to hold a Harvest Festival on Michaelmas Day, as well as on the following Sunday, and there appears to be no reason why we should not do the same at Amberley.'

Outside Constantinople, Constantine not yet dead, there was a church of St Michael that we take to be the first. Another early one was built near Rome, the dedication taking place on September 29th. This date was thereupon adopted for his feast day.

Our warrior archangel, who comes into *Daniel* and *Revelation,* appeared on Monte Gargano between 492 and 496. In Rome, a plague raging, St Gregory saw him sheathe his sword above Hadrian's Tomb, and this huge imperial pile has ever since been known as Castel Sant'Angelo. Thence the fame of the canonized angel spread to Ireland, whose monks made a cult of him, taking it with them to Britain – and then back to the Continent. Hills and high places are especially keen to be named after him: he is a guard against evil spirits from tumuli and devils out of Pandemonium. In the eighth century he appeared on Mont St Michel. The abbey on its peak once owned his sword and shield.

Commander-in-chief of the celestial armies, Michael is the protector of Israel and of that new Israel, the Church. He is the patron saint of mariners, of roentgenologists and of Italy's public discipline and security.

It is possible that the dedication of an earlier Amberley Church was not to Michael but to a Saxon saint, in which case the Normans would have had no compunction about changing it.

The Village

Visitors who approach Amberley from the B2193 will come first upon the village and its school, then the church, and finally the castle. If, however, they have caught the train from Victoria, they need only look out of the left-hand window to glimpse all three simultaneously – the castle (one of England's most perfect sights), beyond it (but only just) St Michael's Church, and, beyond that, the village. All three are strung out along the escarpment that serves as a foot to the Downs and as a wall against floods.

In the foreground are the Wildbrooks, wetlands that may demand stout boots at all times, but, the Arun having been embanked, one cannot, as in winters past, count on rowing across them. Even at high tide – and after the heaviest rain – they are seldom flooded throughout, though by moonlight one may be beautifully deceived into thinking so.

The village, comparatively speaking, is its old self. Geese continue to give their passable imitation of hounds in full cry. The number of inhabitants is between five and six hundred, and so it has been for centuries.

Within ten minutes' walk from the station you will catch your first head-on sight of Amberley: the castle granary, the castle barn, the castle itself, the church and the vicarage. By day they are a procession of stone, brick, flint and tile. At dusk they become an extra down, albeit angular – unlike the cottages, whose thatch undulates no less than the land.

Lanes wind. So, to this day, does the road up the Mount to Downs Farm, though 'horse power' has come to mean something different. Meantime Antonia Maas continues to drive her 1910 wagonette.

15

The village is no longer a huddle of farms; but even in 1900 it contained ten; in 1950 five.

The last was sold for redevelopment in 2000.

Pigs in consequence have disappeared; but Hog Lane is still Hog Lane, and why not? Cattle at least are still driven along it, and sheep-bells still hang from the ceiling of the Black Horse. It is other names – 'High Street', 'Church Street', 'The Square' – that raise a smile; and yet well into the twentieth century they scarcely sounded incongruous: enough trades were still being plied to give the impression of a town in miniature. And today? Forge Cottage, though horseshoes and pairs of pincers lie only a dig beneath the well-kept garden, says nothing of the cartwheels that once debouched onto the roadway. The forge itself is a surgery: it was bequeathed to the village by Dr Pepper, whose family owned the chalk pits, now the Amberley Working Museum.

    *   *   *

Gone are Mr Cooter, baker and churchwarden, who made deliveries by pony and cart; Mr Bacon, minister of the sometime Congregational Chapel, who cobbled shoes of all denominations, and laid out their wearers when they died; and Mr Greenfield, grocer, draper and ironmonger, who sold brooms, brushes, baskets, china, glass, earthenware, flower seed, garden utensils, packed drugs, patent medicines, boots and shoes, clothes, including gentlemen's garments made to order – and hymn books.

Today? A shop we still have, formerly in Southdown House at the lower end of High Street, now in a barn behind it. It is a general stores cum sub-post office. But all those specialist outlets for this or that local produce, or in-house artisanry, are just names of cottages with 'The Old' in front of them.

Will bygone days ever be back? Oh surely! In one shape or another. A harbinger is already with us:

Amberley Pottery, where, as of old,
Pots are thrown and pots are sold.

Founded in 1983, it operates where Mr Bacon once preached.
But the parish of Amberley will never have eight pubs again: we have to make do with three.

St Michael's Church: the Approach

In 681, as a monkish document has it, the turbulent St Wilfrid was favoured by King Caedwalla of the West and South Saxons with various grants of land, including the manor, or parish, of Amberley. Except for church, church hall and vicarage, this is now divided between lay owners, including the castle, which for centuries remained an episcopal residence. Unaltered, however, is the diocesan boundary: it still embraces all Sussex.

Only the bishop's seat has shifted. That was in 1075 – from one-horse Selsea to Chichester, where the Romans, a thousand years previously, had built the forum for what was probably their first military settlement in Britain. Initially they called it 'Noviomagus', the new city of the plain; then 'Regnum', in honour of the local king, Cogidubnus, whom they raised to the rank of Legate. And those masters of everything that may be dignified with the word 'imperial' would surely, had they still been around, have understood the language of construction articulated by those subsequent conquerors, the Normans.

*　　*　　*

17

The Normans had good reason for jettisoning Selsea: the sea's encroachment. But they disapproved in any case of a cathedral's isolation. Better that the bishop were enthroned in a mere parish church, provided it was urban.

A parish church they in fact chose: St Peter's, Chichester. And started improving it forthwith. But only around 1103 did it begin to take on the form that we now recognize as Chichester Cathedral.

What a work! The instigator was Bishop Ralph de Luffa. To him, Norman both in name and energy, we also owe the simultaneous founding of what would grow into Amberley Castle, and, more to the point, the rebuilding of Amberley Church.

Rebuilding is almost certainly the right word. Admittedly nothing of earlier date has been found, but that is unsurprising, the Saxons' favourite material having been cleft trunks of trees; and Wealden oak abounded. But William the Conqueror was determined to re-order the *Ecclesia Anglicana*, and to this project he gave architectural expression – in stone, of course. Or, and especially in Sussex, flint. Rebuilding, whether partial or entire, was the rule. Only the sites tended to remain unaltered.

Whatever Amberley's original church may have been like, at no stage was it large: the holy ground slopes away all too steeply on the north side. Its twelfth-century successor, the nucleus of what we know today, has, true enough, seen expansion, but only to the south, east and west; for although there is a declivity on these sides too, it is slight by comparison.

Too slight, some may carp, to justify a call upon the protection of that celestial friend of prominences, the victorious archangel. Had St Michael been consulted, would he perhaps have vetoed the site, demanding why he had not been allocated the highest point in the village? I doubt it. To tuck himself away within the angle of High Street and The Square! No, thank you. He might never have been found amidst such bosky crannies, whose cottages personify privacy. Our church mound, contrariwise, is something of a landmark, though we must not exaggerate: it is no Mont St Michel, no Sacra di San Michele, not even Tor Hill at Glastonbury or Highgate Hill's top place of worship, which are also dedicated to St Michael; nor does the approach through the village offer any formal perspective: the flag above the tower, invisible from the far end of Church Street, only begins to wave hello from between The Old Brew House and Easter Barton. Hello and *au revoir*: it disappears again behind Panel Cottage, which, with its southern extension beneath a catslide roof, is a little sister of our single-aisled nave. Also akin ('Panel', incidentally, because its half-timber espouses rectilinearity) is the diagonal that divides its front: it rises on the right-hand side from a flight of steps that leads to the right-of-centre front-door, and, still step-like, continues as far as the bedroom windows on the left. Ah, how this aberrant balance subverts the quasi-classical proportions that the eighteenth century conferred upon homespun Tudor!

There was a time when, on drawing level with this little play of symmetry and asymmetry, artists would decide that here was the spot from which to draw the church. Now, however, a copse has grown from the garden of Amberley House,

Deliciously postponing their delight.

Apart from the church tower, the tallest features of the village are its trees. Moreover, while Horsham District Council forbids our buildings to grow taller, it ensures that our trees will continue to do so. And yet – a strange thing, this – we rarely notice them, except from a distance or by night. Nevertheless, they act as a subconscious yardstick whereby we judge the scale of the dwellings, which we accordingly pronounce Lilliputian. And they are indeed small on the whole. Some, needless to say, are larger than others, but not by much.

Even Amberley House is scarcely an exception. If in memory it seems so, that is because it vaunts a slightly grander style: the chimneys, its dominant feature, are corbelled out – and out. So are those of the adjoining Courtyard Cottage, thereby telling us that both cottage and house, originally under single ownership, sprang from the same drawing-board.

An Initial Glance round the Exterior

Church Street culminates, though it does not quite end, in a modest funnelling out. 'Look!' it says, pointing at St Michael's, then veers right, reverently yielding to God's Acre, while ahead stretches the graveyard path.

From this east-south-east angle (one that is prized above all others) the church that the Normans built registers as a mere starting-point for Early English extensions – and for a bit of licence on the part of the nineteenth-century restorer. We are not, that is, looking at the work of a single intellect, far from it, but if we are British we will not care, for we are inured to cumulative architecture. Besides, we welcome anything that may be interpreted as a metaphor for the determining characteristic of our institutions, organic development. To this our retrospective eye may attribute a preconceived unity; and at the turn of the twentieth century there were even architects who designed that curious anomaly, instant tradition – a simulation of piecemeal development. Already, in something of the same vein, not a few Victorian architects had made asymmetry their hallmark. A stylistic quirk? Maybe, but both pragmatic and native.

Complain to an Englishman that Amberley Church is lopsided and he will think you are yourself eccentric. Lopsided? Indeed it is! So is your typical Amberley cottage: this too evolved over centuries, and though the effect is picturesque, the aim was ever down-to-earth.

Am I saying that Amberley Church is only some kind of cottage? What, with tower, arches, stained glass? – not to mention its sheer scale, a scale that is magnified by the uninterrupted sweep of roof, over nave and single aisle. Some cottage! And yet it blends naturally with the toy village, having tumbling out of the same box.

And how child-friendly is this archetypal English church, the model for every model! Not a sharp point or jagged edge to prick an eye or graze a little hand. And yes, feel free to put it in your mouth: no cusp or crocket, no spire or pinnacle, no brattishing or fastigium. No fear! Not a cross to surmount any of the three gable-ends. At Amberley we keep things simple. Look at the ridges of our thatch: nothing fancy about them. For us a clipped hedge counts as topiary.

Have I forgotten our starlings? As the days shorten, they convert themselves into an edging on the roofs of chancel, nave and porch, even on the tower's pyramidal cap. But harmlessly. Clap, and they dissolve in a puff of cloud.

Behind the chancel there rises the nave, behind the nave the tower. And that is it. No fuss. Rather than decorate, you extend: not only has an aisle been added to the nave under the simplest of monopitched roofs, but a porch to the aisle. Both are south-facing, while there is no northern equivalent. It would be an exaggeration to say that one side is all vertical, the other all diagonal, but the north is nevertheless cliff-like. When viewed from the steeply declining Church Street it seems almost one with the retaining wall of the churchyard. The south side, by contrast, presents the mountaineer with little in the way of a challenge: it consists mainly of a sloping roof whose eave is within jumping distance of the sloping churchyard.

Neither geometer nor ecclesiologist will ever alight upon a succinct manner of describing the overall ground-plan, which, for sheer waywardness, vies with – and comes close to reproducing – that of The Square. Meanwhile the purist frowns because symmetry has given asylum to asymmetry.

But come on! Is not the very terrain lopsided? It manifests the same southward hankering as does the church, *die Sehnsucht nach dem Süden.*

*   *   *

There is a quantity of rust below the right-hand lancet of the east end – it has dripped from the saddle-bars – but none below the central and left-hand ones (none visible, at any rate), having been caught by a row of four tablets that are attached to the undressed stone. These, empathetically, conform to the general southern thrust. Originally there was a fifth, which, you would be justified in assuming, positioned itself to the north of the others, for then they would have been symmetrical. But no! It was to the south of the southernmost one, to be removed by the Victorians when they added clasping buttresses.

You will consider me far-fetched if I ask you to recall Raphael's *Alba Madonna*. But hang it in your mind beside this view of our church, and you will note how the south tugs at both – *downwards*, if you will allow me the pun: to the left the central mass declines, but the left is also where the hills are. The river valley is on the right.

Moreover, our eyes cannot dwell on the lancets in the east wall of the chancel without being drawn southwards to a further one in the east end of the aisle. As intended. Or so I believe, for the single lancet in the east end of the south aisle has been designed (if only since the reparation of 1864) to match the three in the east end of the chancel: it is of the same proportions as the central one and of the same height as those on either side. We are consequently induced to interpret the windows as an asymmetrical group of four, no less than as a symmetrical group of three, plus an isolated one, equally symmetrical.

Near the porch is a yew. In 1742, when still a sapling, she was transplanted from the vicarage garden to within a few paces of the porch, whose sentinel she must once have seemed; but now, higher than the roof of the nave and only a little lower than the parapet of the tower, she serves as the church's natural equivalent. The most painted tree in Amberley, she takes up little less of the watercolourist's picture-plane than nave, tower, chancel and porch together.

She? Yes, *she.* That this taxus baccata, to give her her Latin name, is female becomes clear enough in autumn, when she puts on 'oozing, too-soft tassel-berries' – until they drop, transforming the white of an altar-tomb's ledger into the most brilliant of reds. But her trunk is hollow. In 1915 three of her branches broke under the weight of snow. In 1966 a woman called on the vicar, asking him if she could put something in the box for the 'lovely yellow fungus'. He mused that someone might want to buy the nettles at the bottom of the churchyard. But what, I ask, could the parish have bought in recompense for such loss? Nettles say 'country matters'; bring roses to butterflies' cheeks.

> Such sweet neglect more taketh me
> Than all th'adulteries of art.

So our yew was putting forth 'lovely yellow fungus'! Already showing her age. But who am I to talk? Lifelong residents, ones that are even older than me, conserve a childhood memory of rainy days when men were already sheltering inside her; so maybe she will soldier on.

✳   ✳   ✳

To the right of the church, near the foot of the escarpment, nestles Rock

Cottage, whose chimneys scarcely attain the level of the tombstones. And behind stretches the majestic and homely backdrop of the castle.

In the autumn of 1911, a proposal came before the Parochial Church Council to build a lychgate, but in the parish magazine of April, 1912, we read:

> As several of our Parishioners, whose standing as artists demands that their opinions should be seriously taken into account, have expressed themselves averse to the proposal of erecting a Lych-gate, we have abandoned the project.
>
> As a Gate of some kind will have to be put up presently, we have acted on the suggestion of Mr [Edward] Stott to have something similar to the present erection, and have asked the architect to furnish a new design. A Lych-gate would hide the Church too much when viewed from the street.

Designed by W. D. Caroë, ARIBA, of Messrs Caroë & Passmore, and made by Mr Price Allen, the new oaken gates – new-old, one might say – were in place by the autumn. Already, it is quite clear, the view of Amberley Church from the east-south-east was little less than sacrosanct. Indeed it is the most characteristic and informative one, enabling us to read the entire composition. From this side, moreover, we can, with luck, decipher some of the headstones: they all face east, except, understandably, those along the eastern edge.

> Inscriptions here of various Names I view'd,
> The greater part by hostile time subdu'd.

Unsurprisingly, artists' easels have voted this angle the incomparable one, and no one will disagree, except, perchance, the shades of those bishops who for centuries called Amberley Castle their own.

Amberley Castle! Amberley is not a village that acquired a castle but a castle that acquired a village.

An Initial Glance round the Exterior

Oh, did I hear you question the word 'castle'? Fortified manor, then.

People ask why St Michael's was sited where Church Street dwindles, first into a lane, then into a track, finally into a footpath. Why not at the centre? Well, the word 'centre' implies something circular, whereas Amberley is linear; and the line in question – one that no ruler has drawn – begins with the irregular parallelogram of the castle, continues through the eccentrically axial church and ends with the ever-lengthening meander of what is in essence a one-street village. The church, so viewed, is the middle link. True, it is closer to the castle than to the first of the cottages, and far from the last; but the castle is the manor house, and the lord of the manor decided, not altogether atypically, to suit his own convenience. What, he would like to know, is the church if not an integral part of his domain?

The lord of the manor of Amberley, being the bishop of the diocese, had a special justification for adopting this proprietorial attitude. When divine service required his presence in the parish church, he made his way, already vested, across the graveyard at its narrowest point, entering the sacred edifice by the west door. *His* door. And the path that led to it from this most delightful of his country residences belonged to him, too.

A path, no more. Scarcely even that. But, however modest, it has never been blocked, not even in 1379, when Bishop William Rede built that great curtain wall round what had hitherto been simply a country house; for today, as ever, there is a judiciously placed postern.

'Postern' (*janua posterula*) means 'back door', even if, as here, it is a side one. Singularly unpretentious, as if made for pawns rather than prelates, it rises to a four-point arch of perpendicular gothic. But rough-hewn. Oh, it has its attraction, right enough, but largely because of what the weather has inflicted upon it, not because it harboured any other aim than to ensure its own survival beneath the weight of so much wall: it belongs to a home where defence was paramount, though the master mason, one imagines, may possibly have been reproved for constructing so mean an eyelet. In that case he could have been heard to mutter, 'No, 'tis not so wide as a church-door; but 'tis enough, 'twill serve.'

Narrow, it is also low: the voussoirs warn us to mind our heads, which is a sure way of saying 'old'. We can scarcely imagine that it was once a building site, where workmen whistled. And the modern name of 'St Richard's Gate' emphasizes its age, indeed to the point of exaggeration: the canonized Bishop of Chichester died in 1253, so he can never have known it as a mortal man.

But from 1379 his successors did. Their exit through the curtain wall was a kind of entrance to the church, an entrance before the entrance: they were already on holy ground. And in front of them, from that low postern, stretched a gradual revelation. Here, on a more modest scale, as D. H. Lawrence said of Lincoln Cathedral, is 'the light and spring of the great impulse towards the altar.'

Do artists, if only for a change, plant their easels along this solemn route? Very seldom: it is the stuff of cinema, the motion picture, rather than the static art of painting.

*　　*　　*

For us who are not mediaeval bishops there may be the disappointment of finding that the west door and the one between tower and nave are locked. Is there no key to be had? Spare the sexton his pains. Spare yourself yours. Imagine instead what those mighty prelates once experienced, an enfilade. But forget their solemn tread: let your mind advance at a speed that reverence, or, in my case, old age, would deny to flesh and blood. Whiz altarwards. And again! – as waves once did across the Wildbrooks. Go on, treat yourself to a computer-generated fly-through.

An Initial Glance round the Exterior

Was there no drawback to this western approach that bishops alone enjoyed, except during the procession on Palm Sunday? Most definitely there was, for unless, before entering, they had tipped back their mitred heads, little of the exterior would have come into their field of vision. But churches, unlike classical temples, are intended to be seen from within. They may even slot themselves into an office block, like Christ Church, Kennington Road, and still fulfil their function, provided they let us savour the eternity of heaven.

*   *   *

St Michael's stands at the highest point in the immediate vicinity. The floor of the nave, on the other hand, is at ground level, as if to say that the people are of the world, in contrast to the clergy, whose place is in the chancel, where they stand a grading or two higher. Thus the differentiation between church and world in reflected within the church itself.

Reflected and more: the spiritual progression is a double one, not only to a higher level but also eastwards – Easterwards. That is the direction in which the celebrant has always faced, except for periods of disorientation, through one of which we are now passing. Well, our congregation, notwithstanding, continues to face east, and so will our departed on the day of resurrection, which is why they are laid with their heads to the west.

We may conclude (unopposed by the shade of any mediaeval bishop) that the watercolourists' view is not so wonderfully 'right' after all, first because it is westward-looking, secondly because it is an exterior one. This demur gains support from the graveyard path, which, though normally reached from the village, bypasses the chancel, terminating at the west door.

Not that the people would actually have had to walk this far: ever since the present church was built, there has undoubtedly been a south entrance, first in the Anglo-Norman nave, then in the gothic south aisle, and finally through the porch that was added to it.

Added, yes. But an addition it hardly seems, for this gabled access is a necessary conclusion to the drama of the church's southern thrust. It is here, ever since Amberley Castle was made over to a layman, that even Bishops of Chichester have found a convenient point of entry to a church that their predecessors regarded as almost their own peculiar. Here too, until the reign of Edward VI, bridal couples plighted their troth, warmed, we may hope, by the sun, as well as blessed by the clergyman, before whose sign of the cross every devil cowered. And the door on the opposite side of the nave – it had not yet been blocked – was conveniently left open so that the fiendish crew, some said, could the more easily return to the region whence they came - the ill-favoured north.

More prosaically, the porch served as a lobby. It was here that every woman-parishioner left her pattens: before the introduction of pews and hassocks she took care not to muddy the nave floor. And mud abounded in the mediaeval world, not least at Amberley, which in winter could even become waterlogged; so much so that the villagers became known for their webbed feet.

In 1909, however, the lanes were asphalted, and so also was the church path, which, without exaggeration, became one of the straightest and levellest things around. 'Keep to it,' the parish magazine commanded from its great height: there was no longer any excuse for straying onto the grass. But did people need to be told this in so many words? 'Keep to me, keep to me,' says the path itself.

If there is still to be any straying, let it be chiefly on the mown alley that descends the slope between graves and cremation plaques, for this provides the best close-up of church and castle together.

Together indeed! So much so that the church, besides being the parishioners' place of regular worship and occasional secular assembly, could have been taken for the castle's exterior chapel, even if of episcopal proportions; and doubtless this was one purpose that it served when the Bishop was in residence – as he frequently was, and not just in summer: it was a manor for all seasons.

*   *   *

Even if you should pay a hundred visits to St Michael's, let them all, I entreat you, include this view from the south; and let one of them, one at least, be by moonlight, ideally when candles are burning in the chancel and electricity is flooding the nave, so that the stained-glass windows are as bright from without as they are by day from within.

*   *   *

South. East. West. Three sides and a single style: Gothic. That the church is in fact earlier, dating back to the Anglo-Norman period, may have already been surmised, but will only emerge in utter clarity on our going round to the north.

Half a second, though. Should not the north have been where we started? Your strict chronologist will say so, as will your seeker after the picturesque, who, however, rather than crane his neck for a close inspection, will follow the descending course of Church Street to its un-street-like conclusion. In front of him stretch the Wildbrooks, the Weald and the curtain wall of the castle. He rounds the village pond, and, while doves fly from their putlog holes, he scans as much of the church as rises from the thatch of Rock Cottage, and as peeps through the trees in the graveyard. He relishes the assortment of materials and the variety of fenestration, while the soffit is his means of measuring that inward bend of the nave as it joins the chancel. A bend? Slight, casual, it hardly counts as a bend: it could be mistaken for a mistake. Be honest, you would have been happier with an angle, a right-angle. That, my dear *aficionado*, you would call architecture. And an angle is what you would have seen if the mason had imported Caen stone, or even made do with Fittleworth, instead of gathering the flints beneath his feet.

＊　　＊　　＊

During summer, in the early hours and late, these northern walls feel the sun. Then it is that their thickness speaks loudest, such is the contrast with the shade inside the surrounds of the various openings.

Especially inside the Romanesque ones.

Anglo-Norman, to be specific. But the generic term 'Romanesque', though rarely used, has advantages, for it not only denotes this style's Roman origins but also its geographical extent.

'Romanesque.' Listen to the sound it makes, so appropriately massive. Scholars tell us that there was originally a touch of sniffiness about that '-esque', if not actual derision. They have yet to convince me. In any event, massiveness was Rome's defining trait, and this is something that England's Norman conquerors never forgot. Having to defend themselves against the natives, who outnumbered them by a hundred to one, these new Romans used architecture to express their overlordship. Within a century, however, the two races had all but merged, so defence, or the expression of it, was no longer the church builder's prime consideration. Oh, there was another invasion, to be sure, again from across the Channel, but it differed in being a purely cultural one, introducing Gothic.

＊　　＊　　＊

Gothic, given time, would become lightness; and light – the antithesis of the style from which it emerged. And every stage of it is represented at Amberley, but chiefly the initial one, which in England, reasonably enough, is called Early English – though in fact it differs no more than somewhat from the French model.

Does the Early English style tell us the direction in which Gothic will head? Indeed! And nowhere more clearly than in the chancel of Amberley Church, which is of such simplicity that it could well have been designed as a visual aid to *First Steps in Architecture*. 'Observe,' it seems to say, 'how I differ from Anglo-Norman: (1) unlike the windows of the nave, mine have a spring to them, rising to a point; (2) they are set lower; (3) they are slightly wider; (4) they are considerably taller; (5) their glass is almost flush with the outside wall; (6) they discard the weighty effect of architectural surrounds, being content with perfectly plain ones – of stone, it is true, but only because flint and rubble are impractical for edging.'

The difference between the two styles, however, is slight enough for Amberley Church to register as a oneness: our Early English is closer to Romanesque than to late Gothic, whose attenuation of solids and enlargements of voids are barely adumbrated. A small step, then? Doubtless. But no mean one. *La distance n'y fait rien: il n'y a que le premier pas qui coûte.*

*   *   *

Rubble and unworked flint in a superfluity of mortaring are a kind of concrete, and they preclude thinness. Therefore, though the nave maximizes the effect of massiveness and the chancel goes some way towards minimizing it, their walls are of identical thickness, one metre, which for a parish church is the Romanesque norm. And the chancel's western two-fifths are actually of Anglo-Norman origin, the vertical straightwork between the middle and western windows being the remains of stone coigns. These, interrupting the flint-work on both the north and south sides, tell us that once upon a time the chancel stretched no further. They tell us, too – and no less obviously – that, though lengthened, it has not been widened.

*   *   *

Had our church's Anglo-Norman builder lived to twice three score years and ten, he would have seen how his proportions had been changed. But though he might have shaken his head, he is unlikely to have advised any compensatory widening, even by straightening and projecting the inward curve at the east end of the nave – first because mediaeval enlargers (except in South Lincolnshire, where funds seem to have been limitless, disruption of no consequence) retained as much of the existing walls as possible; secondly because the chancel, if distinct from the nave, was *de rigueur* slightly narrower, being the head, while the nave was the body; for Christ 'is the head of the body, the church'; and the clergyman is His type and representative, just as the congregation is synecdochic for all faithful people.

Thus, in the early gothic period, when ecclesiastical rituals grew more elaborate, it came about that chancels were lengthened without being widened. The call was simply for more room, more and more room, especially if the church had episcopal connections.

And what if the bishop, as in the case of Ralph Nevill, should happen to be Chancellor of England in his spare time, and also of Ireland, for good measure?

Bishop Nevill had to pilot the ship of state. Churches are ships too, whose port is salvation, and their ground plan can have a naval look to it, especially in France. But English ones are generally more like trains, even if of only two carriages, as at Amberley, with a tower for locomotive, coupled at the rear.

According to P.M. Johnston, it was the priesting of ordinands *en masse* that necessitated the lengthening of our chancel. And I can see his point, especially if they lay prostrate. But is so particular an explanation necessary? English gothic chancels have a marked tendency to be long – on average about two-thirds the length of the nave. The one at Amberley exceeds this, true enough, but may not state have counted more than function?

One thing is certain: in early gothic times feudalism reached its peak, setting the pattern for prelates as well as for barons, indeed for the Pope himself. The lower clergy too, poor though they may have been, were party to the same hierarchism. What, then, if they had to officiate at altars that were far removed from the congregation, with sight-lines that would put a theatre out of business? So be it.

A Closer Look at the Exterior

Sussex prefers its towers to be plain, nor is the one at Amberley an exception: it comes across as yeomanly, quite without airs, and yet confident enough to rub shoulders with the castle on one side and the body of the church on the other. It thus provides a visual link between them. Like the castle, it is more stone than flint, whereas nave and choir are more flint than stone, plus tiled roof; and when the bells look through the louvred opening in their east side, tiles are all they see – plain tiles on a plain gable.

Plain indeed, and yet what a gable and a half! Not grand, however: it scarcely says 'nave': 'tithe-barn' rather. Contemptuous of finery, it bothers even less about symmetry: nothing counts but the job in hand.

And did we not observe a second ago that the tower itself had a workaday air? Instead of 'Stand back and admire,' it just says, 'Stand back!'

Gentlemen, you lay siege to it at your peril.

*   *   *

Unlike the curtain wall of the castle, whose base is scarcely distinguishable from the escarpment, the tower is clearly all tower. None the less, aubretia and valerium forever colonize it as if it were Nature's work rather than Man's. Try dating it with precision. 'Old' is what it says, stylistic clues being meagre; 'age-old', even if it is marginally younger than the chancel extension and the south aisle. We read in *Dear Amberley* (1968) by the Reverend E. Noel Staines, who was our vicar: 'The knapping on the lower part of the tower, below a clearly defined arch of stone work . . . suggests that this was the original early twelfth century work.' Mr Staines does not specifically say that there was a twelfth-century tower, and we may be sure that the original Anglo-Norman plan excluded any such feature, otherwise we would not have the window in the west end of the nave, manifestly built as an external one. The knapped flint to which he refers is found on the upper part of the tower as well as the lower, but on the south side only. It may come from an original part of the castle that was demolished in the thirteenth century. There was to be no further use of knapped flint on any part of the church until the north door was blocked, and that would not have occurred before the Reformation.

At belfry level, on the north, south and west sides, there are two openings: the upper one is rectangular with a moulded lintel, while the lower one, having more weight of wall to bear, is a lancet. On the east side, however, the gable of the nave reaches as high as the sill of the rectangular opening, which is like the ones on the other sides, except that the lintel, being unmoulded, is an obvious replacement, probably dating from the reparation of 1963/4 – on the completion of which the parish magazine commented, 'We can walk about Sion . . . and mark well her bulwarks.' (*Psalm* xxxxviii. 11 and 12) This may sound a touch like over-dramatization, but unless St Michael's is in some measure Jerusalem, it may as well fall. Besides, there was the drama that a centenary never entirely lacks: ' . . . it is going to be possible in 1964 to complete the restoration of Amberley Church – just a hundred years after the great restoration work of the Revd George Clarkson.' (Clarkson's architect was Gordon M. Hills, of John

A Closer Look at the Exterior

Street, The Adelphi, London, his builder Robert Busby of Little-hampton.) The magazine also paid tribute to the Reverend William Champion Streatfeild, who, after an interregnum of five months, succeeded Clarkson on 26th December, 1897, and immediately 'put a very satisfactory finish to the work so thoroughly done years ago to the rest of the fine old building.' Furthermore repairs were undertaken in the late 1940s and early 1950s.

* * *

Across the tower's north side, almost halfway up, stretches a semicircular arch, a sustaining one. Of the plainest. Semicircular? What, you enquire, can the master mason have been up to, Goth that he was? But he would disclaim any stylistic intent. 'It's semicircular because it's semicircular.' 'Observe, sirrah,' you insist, 'how it harmonizes with the Anglo-Norman openings in the nave.' The bluff fellow only shrugs. You hesitate, then decide to leave it at that. For who are you to argue?

You make your way round to the south side. There, not unexpectedly, you find a second sustaining arch. But it is no twin – not, at any rate, an identical one: it is pointed. Why pointed? The bluff fellow would doubtless reply that it's pointed because it's pointed. But wait a minute: other arches on the south side are pointed, too. Sheer chance? Or was a sensitive soul at work?

There is no answer at the back of the book.

On the west side a third sustaining arch thought that if it was to squeeze itself with tolerable comfort between the door and the window which is 1.11 m above it, it had better be segmental. Its purpose is to strengthen – or, strictly speaking, strengthen further – the lower part of the wall, which is thicker than the upper part, the set-off being edged with stone. We could thus say, without too severe a misuse of language, that in effect the whole width of wall is buttressed.

Buttresses – this time the word needs no apology – jut from the north-west and south-west corners. Being diagonal, they must date from the Decorated period, hence they are a later addition to the Early English tower. But no less austere. So to call them 'Decorated' (comfortably though the word sits on Exeter Cathedral, to take the prime example, and even on Amberley Church's south door) may seem risible. However, the chief characteristic of this mid-gothic style is not decoration as such, but movement. And movement in the instance of these two buttresses is conveyed by their encroachment on the surrounding yard. This is peculiarly trenchant in that they constitute the only departure from approximate rectilinearity throughout the entire ground plan.

Similarly their contours, being a zigzag of set-offs and uprights, may count as diagonal in their overall thrust. And what thrust! One senses the need for a heftier word than 'buttress' if one is to convey the elbowing impact of these two hobbledehoys. Hardly less tall than the nave, they provide the body of the church with a visual counter-weight. Their intention, however, was doubtless more practical: abutment against vibration that arose from the increase in the number and size of bells.

If the conveyance of movement reached its peak in Decorated, it had been discernible from the moment when Gothic started questioning the fundamentals of that most static of styles, Romanesque. Romanesque, understandably, had no great love of the diagonal: it was happy to strengthen walls with mere pilaster-strips.

Pilaster-strips always rise parallel with the wall, like the pair against the north-west corner of our nave. These, however, are Romanesque only in style, not in date, judging by the condition of the stone. They were probably erected during the reparation of 1864, and almost certainly *de novo:* a drawing of 1818 omits them. And yet, though they only jut 30 cm from the wall, they are considerable structures, being one metre wide, equal to the thickness of the walls.

Would it be an exaggeration to suggest that they might themselves be taken for wall? Hardly in the case of the west-facing one: it reaches so close to the north-west corner of the tower that a chimney, slender though it is – as slender as tall, even topping the unembattled belfry – fills the entire interstice. Of smooth brick, with chamfered angles, it clings to the rough-and-ready stone, a tendril climbing an oak. It was erected at the beginning of Lent, 1907, as part of the heating system. It cost £6.13.8. Initially it gave trouble, being insufficiently high. In the following year it was raised further at the cost of an additional £10. Having now outlived its practical purpose, however, it is deemed a parasite and may be torn from its host. In that case the pilaster-strip that flanks it will be able to breathe a little more easily, having recovered some space – not a great deal, it has to be said: only half its own width, neither more nor less. But does that not suggest a nice regard for proportion?

You are saying – I can hear you – that the strip will still be cramped. But you are too hasty in your condemnation. Bear in mind that the original west façade has been largely obscured by the addition of the tower.

'The tower!' you retort. Adding: 'If the twin pilaster-strips are its junior – its junior indeed by six centuries – does not the charge of disproportion remain unparried?' Well, Mr Hills would point out that the style in which he designed them was an anterior one, Anglo-Norman. So let us try pretending to ourselves – no insuperable task – that they are authentic. After all, gothic additions were rarely seamless joins. What we have condemned as disproportionate may then charm us as quaint.

In 1960 a boiler room for oil-fired heating was built against the north wall of the tower. Of precast concrete blocks, it was egregiously left unclad. Flints would have been a softening. Its affinity is not with the church walls, except in so far as it extends their range of materials – wide already – but with the metal tank in front of it.

Oh, you admire these two additions, do you? Their similarity and difference. You will tell me that they are a sculptor's minimalist interpretation of the original two-cell church; or simply commend their honesty. Fine, as long as you attribute no such virtue to the cost-cutting members of the Parochial Church Council, who had no interest in functionalism, only function.

* * *

The two original windows of the nave's north side have a triple surround, which is quite an extravagance for a village church. The outer ring, in typical Romanesque fashion, must originally have been enlivened by a regular alternation of red and white ashlar, but this has grown random in the course of reparation. The middle ring is set back; the inner one is much narrower and set back even further.

We may argue that these recessions achieve a false perspective, *i.e.*, that the wall appears to be thicker than it actually is. The plaster which originally covered the walls, moreover, simulated solid stone, and this illusion was reinforced by the edging of genuine ashlar.

Churches of flint and rubble were so regularly coated in plaster that though our walls show no trace of it I would have felt justified in stating that ours was no exception, even if there had been no evidence to which I could point. But there is: in *Notes on Amberley* (1865) Clarkson writes of the reparation that had just been completed: 'Among the works of 1864–65, are, with respect to the chancel, the cutting into it and the erection of buttresses at its north-east and south-east angles, the removal of plaster and roughcast externally, the reparation and pointing of the north and south walls ... '

In the Middle Ages, therefore, the exterior walls looked much less 'mediaeval' than they do today. Perhaps we like them the way they are. In *Sussex* (1947) Reginald Turnor pronounces that our church 'is one of the best I know, with a fine Norman chancel-arch and nave-windows, and, outside, a superlatively soft and beautiful texture.' The Normans, however, would have deplored our preference. They wanted their village church to evoke imperial Rome, its coat of plaster to suggest – ideally – marble. A statement of overlordship, it was to stand out from the neighbouring dog-houses of the English.

On the other hand it was probably thatched with Arun reed. And what could be more vernacular than that? Might it then be that I am exaggerating the Roman link? That would be difficult. Our idea of Rome was formed by the Renaissance, which looked back to pagan Augustus, but let us not anachronistically impose such a perspective on the Anglo-Normans: for them Rome at its summit was a Christian one, that of the basilica at Trier. In the second half of the seventh century St Wilfrid was importing workmen from a Rome already barbarized. And what we call the Carolingian Renaissance was for Charlemagne a *renovatio*, a renewal. Rome reborn? She had never died.

Between the two Anglo-Norman windows there is a door that attains the level of their sills. It is blocked, and probably has been since the Reformation, when processions were considered a wearing away of clogs to no good purpose. In the upper third there is a window. The rest has been walled up and faced with a chequer of stone and knapped flint. The fact that such trouble was taken to achieve a decorative effect tells us that there had been no intention of plastering it.

A door, and what a door! Like the windows, it is Anglo-Norman, but on an even grander scale: indeed, the arch has so thick a roll-moulding that our eyes require it to have two nook-shafts in support. As it originally did. But, bar their plinths, they survive not, hence we may judge them to have been purely decorative, no structural problems having ensued.

Did I say 'decorative'? Decorative but not meaningless, for these marks of authority carry the idea of Roman permanence. Thus it was that the Norman rulers expressed their own Caesarism: the north door of a village church in inaccessible Sussex became their version of a triumphal arch. At the same time, and no less so, it was reasserting the supremacy of the Roman pontiff, whom the Great Schism of 1054 had finally detruded from eastern Christendom, and whose commands, alas, the wilful and insular English had tended to treat as suggestions.

It is quite in character that the Normans should have built so robust a church within thirty-five years of their arrival, but not till later can the openings have acquired their present grandeur. Or so one may assume; and the stylistic evidence supports this: the surrounds must date from after the Great Anarchy of Stephen's reign (1134–54), and their greater width necessitated the heightening of the original nave wall, the top metre of which is markedly different – of stone, not flint and rubble.

Five and a half centuries later, a different type of opening was pierced, one that specifically threw extra light on the pulpit at the east end of the nave. Its frame is basically rectangular, a rationalistic development from the Perpendicular window in the south aisle. It takes the shape of an open book, which is not inappropriate, its aim being to ensure that the parson should see clearly as he read the service from the pulpit. He may also have read his sermon, but we would prefer that he spoke *memoriter*.

Almost as wide as it is high, this extra window, an obvious inter-loper, makes little attempt to seem ecclesiastical. The English had gradually flattened the arch out of existence: they were on holiday from church-building.

Come was the era of Shakespeare's 'gorgeous palaces', and (to compare great things with small) of this pulpit-window. Slightly recessed and with no surround to speak of, it could easily have strayed from one of the older cottages. The mullion that divides it, moreover, is of the plainest. Square in section, but set diagonally, it derives from Perpendicular. Above the moulded lintel, by contrast, there is a segmental pediment, announcing that the Renaissance has reached Amberley. Architecturally, Latin was succeeding English to become the language of the Reformation. An arch, barely an arch and innocent of rhetoric, it contrasts with the *Book of Common Prayer*'s cadenced Ciceronianism – applied, moreover, to a barbarian window.

A barbarian window that is set asymmetrically, moreover. As long as the Anglo-Norman openings were the nave's only ones, they must have resembled two eyes and a mouth: there was a beauty of balance – only to be scuppered by this newcomer. Just look at it! A rectangle! – with no surround worthy of the name. Furthermore, it is a little low, and, worse, broad enough for a man to climb through, even without his having removed the single mullion. It thus casts doubt on Mother Church as a stronghold, as a refuge in time of trouble, and it bates her role as a house of altar and sacraments, alluding instead to the primacy of words. Indeed, it is itself a sermon.

And quite rightly, you will say. It is an addition, and of its age – an age when Calvinists and Jesuits concurred that preaching should no longer be left to friars. Nor did the Anglican clergy dissent from this view. But the Virgin Queen, despite her injunction that all parish churches should possess 'a comely and honest pulpit', had her eye on them: she feared dissenting voices, whether Roman or Genevan. Certainly few Elizabethan pulpits have survived, if that is anything to go by. Our window may therefore date from no earlier than the year 1603, when James I, having barely reached his English throne, likewise commanded that there should be a pulpit in every church. And a Jacobean one, or, as in our case, neo-Jacobean, has become the norm.

The people who knocked this hole in the ancient edifice had more important things on their minds (need I say?) than the pattern of fenestration. They may even have argued that in actual fact they had abused no symmetry because there had been no symmetry to abuse; and certainly a careful look at the Anglo-Norman openings will reveal that those eyes (as I have chosen to call them) are not equidistant from the mouth, the one on the left being a span farther away. Why such randomness? To all appearances the pulpit-window was to exercise some magnetic force, but, Johnny-come-lately as it is, it can hardly have been the determinant factor. None the less, we may rejoice that it serves as a hyphen between nave and chancel: it so links the two disparate elements that they may be read as a single compound. Viewed thus, does its asymmetrical placing not seem rather sensitive? Some may deplore that after those centuries of the pointed arch it has brought us back to earth; but the landing was a gentle one: the defining Christian virtue, humility, is still at home here, despite the advent of humanism.

This is the sole window in the entire body of the church that can never have known stained glass, and the nineteenth-century lattice-work is probably a mere replacement of what was there originally – except for the two vertical bars that rise to a fleur-de-lys. We find the same in the central east window. The Victorian aesthete loved such embellishments. He also enjoyed attaching symbolic significance to them, in this case the Holy Trinity.

Concerning the reparations of 1864, Clarkson refers, with an irksome want of elaboration, to 'the blocking up of a north window.' This, on the evidence of a drawing made in 1788 and reproduced in *Dear Amberley,* was over the north door.

*   *   *

And now let us consider the three lancets in the north wall of the chancel. Their asymmetry, as with the matching ones to the south, is unmistakable. But not inexplicable: if there is an especially wide stretch of blank wall to the west of the north-east and south-east corners, this is because the east end, with three lancets of its own, amply lights the adjacent area without recourse to help from the sides. The logic of this is as clear as daylight. And the practice common. But why should the central window in both the north and the south sides not be equidistant from those to the east and west of it? Answer: to avoid breaking into the vertical line of coign-stones that interrupts the flint. These reinforced a corner of the original chancel, which in all probability ended in a semicircular apse: Ian Nairn, in the 'Sussex' volume of *Buildings of England*, points to the shortness of the masonry in the flat end of the Early English extension.

* * *

Farther to the west there is another vertical line of stones. These, being only half a metre from the junction with the nave, can never have formed part of a coign: they were doubtless intended as a strengthener. Observe how there is no equivalent in the south wall, where the aisle makes for more than sufficient stability.

I see you shifting in your chair, sapient reader. The south aisle had not yet been built? But the Anglo-Norman church already broadened at this point – not with a mere curve (and a slight one) as on the north side, but with a rectangular projection, a metre in width, terminated by the south-east corner of the as yet aisle-less nave.

Anglo-Norman and so symmetry-defying? But not without a purpose, which was to allow room for a nave altar.

* * *

You remember how the windows of that long north side dispose themselves: two of them Anglo-Norman (not counting the one that has been let into the top part of the blocked doorway), one

Elizabethan or Jacobean, and three Early English. Additionally, in syncopation with these groupings, there is a tripartite division of the wall's actual surface: the nave is mainly flint and rubble (I am tempted to say rubble and flint); the chancel, from the junction with the nave as far as the straightwork between the middle and eastern windows, is flint that shows signs of coursing; and then, from the straightwork to the north-east corner, it rejects this disorderly order for orderly disorder, becoming a dance before our eyes. Not a formal ballet. But people mafficking. Their territory, clearly defined, is the chancel extension of 1230, but they themselves, flitting on its surface, date only from the reparation of 1864. By then there would have been no question of covering it with plaster: they are themselves a rendering: they render dance, one without end. Aesthetic? We must not exaggerate. It is as far from flushwork as Sussex from East Anglia: here is no refinement, only a charivari, an art of nature. We delight, however, in the even unevenness of beautiful materials and in a job well done – by local labourers who were doubtless accustomed to restoring the odd cottage. Unversed in anything we would call architecture, they were a different breed from those craftsmen, probably French, who built our Anglo-Norman openings, and, in their spare time, Chichester Cathedral.

I must ask you to store this dance of flint in your mind's yes, for I shall be referring to it again when we reach the south side. And not only that but also the horizontal lines of stones that are embedded in the wall.

Rounding the corner, we leave flints behind, except that they peep, as gallets, from the odd crevice. Bar that, the east end is of undressed greenstone. In it are set three lancets. Unlike those in the chancel's side walls, they are symmetrically placed. As we would expect! On the other hand we may ask ourselves why the central one, which rises only slightly higher than those on either side, should be disproportionately broader.

Worse, and quite contrary to the norm, the amount of wall that divides them exceeds that which flanks them. Before we blame the Early English builders, however, we should take the clasping buttresses into account: these, of ashlar, only date from 1864. They are neo-gothic additions to a genuinely gothic part, just as those neo-Romanesque ones were additions to a Romanesque part. So far so consistent. But imagine this east wall as it originally was: unbuttressed. You will then be left in no doubt that its proportions were once happier. Far from perfect, however, if those three lancets were exactly as they are now.

East-end lancets, not just in Sussex but throughout the country, are generally bunched. Divided by mere mullions, they form, as it were, the lights of a single window, one that rises step-like to an apex, thus offering a happy variant on the shape of the gable-end in which it is set. At Amberley such kinship would have been particularly effective, for the roof of the chancel is at the same pitch as that of the nave, with a chevron of wall between them. Instead, what we actually have is three windows that could be misread as identical – especially as they are so far apart. Not that I am begging them to cuddle up: by keeping their distance they happily accord with those in the lateral walls, and this will fully emerge when we go inside: we shall then see all nine simultaneously. There they are, inhabiting a sequence of splayed recesses which Clarkson happily calls 'arcadic'.

*   *   *

On the cover is a sketch of Amberley Church, dated 1859, by a certain Dr Rickarts. He chose the east-south-east angle, and, less conventionally, an early hour, so that the south-facing walls are in shade. Furthermore, the nave casts a triangular shadow on the aisle, as does the aisle on the porch, creating diagonals that seem to take their cue from those of the roofs. This is artful, as is also the touch of the pen – artfully rustic: a village church and churchyard have become an idyll.

Idylls of the King came out in the year this sketch was drawn. So, for that matter, did *Critique of Political Economy*. Oh, and the first oil well was being drilled; work began on the Suez Canal; Kaiser Bill was born. And in our humble churchyard, if Rickarts may be trusted, a yokel was squatting on an altar-tomb beside the as yet unasphalted path.

Today's topographer would be obliged to include telegraph poles, but otherwise the modern world has barely encroached. The chief changes, ironically enough, have been to the church itself. As long as the northern and southern windows had been substantially lower than the central one, the trio had risen to an apex – not parallel to the gable-end of the chancel, it is true, but near enough to suggest sympathy with it, and (it follows) with that of the nave, too. But Clarkson raised the side ones to little less than the height of the middle one. He thus created more light. But he deprived them of a clear relationship with each other. Though the three have not become identical, we could be forgiven for believing that they were. Further-more, the middle lancet, now that the side ones are so very little lower, cannot justify its considerably greater width. It needs to slim a bit.

We learn from Rickarts' pen-and-ink sketch that these windows, though lancets, were treated to round-headed surrounds. It is strange that Early English builders should have done such a thing. We might even consider the possibility of artistic licence on the part of this gifted doctor, but we have no need, for there is a pencil drawing by Adelaide Tracy, dated June 2nd, 1850, that tells the same story. So the surrounds of the windows in the original apse must have been recycled. They lasted till the reparation of 1864.

Like them or not, I hear you tut-tut that Clarkson should have dispensed with an element of such antiquity; but Romanesque found little favour with the Victorians: they tended to regard it as primitive, at best conceding that Gothic sprang from it. For its subsequent return to favour we must thank modern art, which, to some extent, is primitivism revisited.

*   *   *

On the chancel's south wall, very close to the corner, there was once a tablet, identical to those on the east wall. It can be seen in Tracy's drawing. Like its neighbour round the corner, it had to be removed in 1864 when the clasping buttresses were added.

Basically the differing surfaces of the chancel's south wall mirror the north. However, the easterly section has been diversified by the inclusion of quite large buff stones. I take them to be Pulborough sandstone, which can scarcely be cut small. These, being somewhat evenly distributed, enjoy the same disorderly order that we have already observed in the flints. That they were considered a further embellishment is clear from their having been set exclusively in the south side, the one we all see. With this in mind, I feel confident in saying that the two lines of horizontal stones, four in each, also date from the reparation of 1864. I asked you, you will remember, to retain a picture of those on the north side: the easterly one, of four stones, is symmetrical with the one in the south wall, and so would the westerly one be, except that it is interrupted by the straightener near the junction with the nave, leaving room for only two stones. But there is another difference, and this a fundamental one: the six on the north side are just superior rubble, whereas the eight on the south fall barely short of ashlar.

A pattern is at work, therefore, on these two stretches of wall: better materials are reserved for the southern one.

Obviously this facing cannot be the work of mediaeval masons. Why should they have taken the trouble to create an effect that would be plastered over? And those lines of horizontal stones cannot originally have been the lintels of square-headed doors for vicar and bishop: a long single one would have been required in each case. I believe our Victorian restorer, contemporary of Darwin, saw our church with the eyes of an evolutionist rather than a creationist. His lintels are fictitious? Yes, but he employed them in the way that a historical novelist would have done, hinting at doors that he quite justifiably assumed were once there. Four at any one time is unfeasible, but he was doubtless positing two for the Anglo-Norman chancel (one for the vicar, one for the bishop) and another two for the Early English extension.

*   *   *

In drawing the east end, Rickarts is helpful enough to include the latticed lancets within the round-headed surrounds. But the south side of his chancel is so deeply shaded that its windows are half lost. Let us be grateful, then, for Tracy's amateurishly emphasizing them: there can be no doubt that their surrounds are as round-headed as those in the east end. On the other hand she offers us no sign of the lancets within them. That they already existed before the reparation of 1864 is clear from the print of 1820 and confirmed by Clarkson in *Notes on Amberley.*

If the original chancel, short though it was, had two further round-headed windows, one on either side, these could have been retained when it was extended, and, as in the east end, filled with lancets. But the Early English extenders required two more lancets on either side. To these they gave round-headed surrounds – from scratch. It follows that Amberley Church, between the years 1230 and 1864, must have had the earliest example of Neo-Romanesque in Europe.

Does this seem unlikely? Then look at the alternative. Build pure lancets and see them outnumbered four to five by ones in round surrounds! And then there were the windows in the nave, all round-headed too – if the south aisle had not yet been built. But in *Dear Amberley* Noel Staines believes that it had. Acknowledging a debt to J. L. Denman he writes: ' . . . the general appearance of the arcade suggests that the south aisle belongs to an earlier period of architecture. The griffes at the foot of the pillars suggest a late twelfth century style rather than thirteenth. The actual entry in Bishop Rede's Register reads, "The same person (Bishop Nevill died in 1252) built anew the chancel of the Church at Amberley." It does not mention the south aisle or Tower.'

The earlier date would take us back to the very beginning of English Gothic, when most masons had been apprenticed in the Anglo-Norman style. The pointed arch, in their eyes, would have been a logical development from the round-headed one, not a break. The concept of Gothic was as unknown to them as the word, its development unimagined.

✻ ✻ ✻

Whereas the chancel's north wall, allowing for that slight bend, is continuous with the nave's, there is a right-angle at the western end of the south one, the whole length of which, therefore, we may observe in isolation. We are therefore better placed to mark the difference of surface to the right and left of the straightwork. If, however, we fail to do so, that is because of the much starker contrast afforded by the east wall of the south aisle: quite without warning it entertains us with a veritable anthology of local materials. It may even remind us of Amberley's older cottages.

The angle of the chancel and the south aisle is of stone. As one would expect. But at certain levels, especially that of the chancel eave, it extends further to the left than the actual corner-stones. Here, I would suggest, are the remains of an original Anglo-Norman wall. It consisted of stones because it was only one metre wide, that is to say it stretched as far as the south-east angle of what was then an aisle-less nave. I feel confident, let me add, that it had a window in it, small though it must have been, to light the nave altar. Like all openings, it would have required stone edging. There is no longer any sign of it, the wall having been resurfaced, but in Tracy's drawing there is a window further to the left, exactly where we now have a lancet. And a lancet it must already have been, only she has declined to drawn it: as in the chancel, she has confined herself to a round-headed surround. I ask myself whether this may not derive from the original Anglo-Norman window, enlarged and re-erected further to the south.

Would we be rash in assuming that this round-headed surround lasted until the reparation of 1864, to be replaced by the present lancet? Rash not. Simply mistaken. In the sketch of 1859 it is an ogee! Now, the ogee is an Arabic arch that was adopted by the English in the fourteenth century, then revived during the Regency. But St Michael's was acquiring one in the 1850s. This is so bizarre that we may again question whether Rickarts' pen should be trusted. I think so: The Manse (1883), next door to Amberley Village Pottery, was designed to include windows in the Indian style that came from the Brighton Pavilion. Historians – mark my words – will one day be writing about Victorian Sussex's 'Regency Revival'.

Although, you remember, the projection on the north side of the nave constitutes only the slightest of bends, it is nonetheless the visible one in that no north aisle was ever added – visible rather than obvious, being materially little different, just our familiar flint and rubble.

The greater projection on the south side would not as such have excluded the possibility of using flint and rubble: a quadrantal curve we find in St Mary and All Saints, Newton-by-Castle Acre – and in farm buildings. But here, as I have said, there was to be a nave altar against the inside surface, so only a right-angle would do; and right-angle means stone – never flint and rubble at any rate. This projection was quadrupled in width by the addition of the south aisle, whose east wall especially stands out because some of it has been faced with brownish stone. None other of this hue is visible from the south-east, only the prevailing greenstone, but there is some in the north wall; also around the west end, where it has chiefly been used for coigns.

Here, however, there is a uniquely large area of it.

Can stones have fancy? I ask this because they seem to have diverted themselves in creating a silhouette of the castle's ruined enceinte. A 'mural' in the most literal sense of the word! But this cannot have had their intent: the castle survived intact until the seventeenth century. No, a mediaeval *jeu d'esprit* it is not. In fact it is not mediaeval at all: we are looking at stones that have only been here since 1938, the year in which Hitler occupied the Sudetenland. I can hear the builders saying, 'We decided on a distinguishable stone because we wouldn't like you to take it for original. This is a patch-job, designed to combat the damp that was affecting the south side of the chancel arch.' (They would shortly be engaged in a different kind of combat.)

How ironical that this twentieth-century workmanship (so seemingly crazy – or picturesque, you may think) should strike us as farthest from all that is modern! Doubly ironical in that it would have found scant favour with the original builder, who, as I have reminded you, took the trouble to plaster over the external walls, even those that displayed a far less anarchic diversity of materials. This one (raise your eyes!) even sports three beams. What can they be doing up there? They have the casual look of an opportunistic addition, so we might justifiably assume that a waste-not-want-not workman, having chanced upon them, decided they should be incorporated. But the uppermost one (which you may already have noticed from the north side) is a collar-beam of the nave gable. And the other two? They form a reverse L. This, in the absence of a clerestory, provides the sole external clue to a structural divide that we shall encounter on entering the church: an arcade that replaced the south wall of the nave when the aisle was added.

This east wall of the south aisle is the only one with exposed timbers on its external side. Moreover, it is stepped, the lower three-fifths being thick, the upper two as thin as flint and rubble will allow. The Romans – let us give them due credit – had already built thus, at Pevensey Castle, and if ever I run into them I shall say how tickled I am that they had such close followers a thousand years after their departure. And they will reply, 'Maybe, dear colonial, but I'm unhappy about that set-off. One would think that daedal Nature had turned an unaccustomed hand to masonry. Better it were edged with stone, like the one of the west side of the tower, if only to justify the corresponding kink in the edge of the nave roof.' I can hardly believe my ears. Would they want to do the plasterer out of a job?

*   *   *

Let us now turn to the aisle's south wall. At eye-level, scratched into a coign-stone, is a mass-dial. The gnomon is missing from its hole.

Moving westwards, we come first upon a double lancet, whose surround is incomparably more worn than those of all our other gothic windows. The glass and leading, however, appear twentieth-century, as indeed they do throughout the church. And in the parish magazine for February, 1915, we read: 'The Ecclesiastical Commissioners have agreed, after an application by the Vicar, to put in five new windows in the Chancel, and execute other repairs. Nearly all the windows in the Church are very old, and the lead work has perished, allowing wind and rain to come through.'

*   *   *

We turn next to the porch, which, paving stones apart, is Victorian. Clarkson tells us that it was previously 'covered with Horsham stone, the like material, within the last twenty-five years, lying on the lower part of the south roof. It bore the date 1637. Its demolition took place on Whit-Monday, 1865, to make way for another since erected, more worthy of the pointed arch, and of the carved foliage, at the inner doorway.'

The stone dated 1637 was built into the Church Hall of 1964. Set above a Victorian letter-box, it was two years old when services for the carriage of public correspondence were established. Moreover, it had reached the age of twenty when the mail service became a parliamentary responsibility, and it celebrated its bicentenary in the year when the Queen who was destined to become Empress of India ascended the throne of England.

Rickarts' sketch gives us some idea of the porch that Clarkson demolished: its gable reached scarcely a hand's breadth above the eave of the great roof, whereas the present one is about a metre higher. Otherwise it seems to have been similar in general shape and doubtless evoked something of a gothic feel. But that was not enough for the Victorians, who have produced a scholarly rendition of Early English, the chief feature being the façade. A pair of columns, cylindrical with moulded capitals, and the double-chamfered arch that rises from them, doubtless derive from the genuinely thirteenth-century arcade of the south aisle. But perforce finials had to be added, one to either spring of the arch. And the ashlar at the corners, as generous as wayward, leaves areas of flint, interspersed with undressed stone, mirroring the eastern section of the chancel's south wall, except that the areas are small and eccentric. Nor is there symmetry between one side and the other. Along the sides are footings, all right on Chichester Cathedral but out of place in Amberley, high heels in a meadow. And they are not even the same, the eastern one being so low that there is little room for wall below the set-off. What is this if not a skit on the catslide roof? Always this quest for the quirky. You have seen heads in flints before, all of them grotesque, but on either side of the entrance to the porch there are so many that the mason must have gone around collecting them. Maybe he thought they would compensate for the absence of gargoyles.

You dislike these flints? Find them Victorian? They are as old as those the Anglo-Normans laid, for they all date from the Cretaceous Era, which ended seventy million years ago. Blame the wormily trowelled ribbon pointing and the use of cement mortar. Turn your eyes to the right and glance at the south aisle. Observe the difference.

We are now inside the porch. The pavement that the restorers laid includes re-used stones, fragments with lettering that Clarkson dates, rather wildly, to the twelfth or thirteenth century.

There is also the indent of a small, monumental brass, broken in two, which was removed from the chancel when tiles were laid. But one slab, of Portland stone, has only ever been in its present position: designed by J. W. Cooper, ARIBA, who lived at Martins, it is in the far right-hand corner. The inscription reads:

1911–1980
IN LOVING MEMORY
BRIAN JAMES ROBERTS
ROBERTS
AIR COMMODORE R.A.F.
12 SQUADRON
BOMBER COMMAND
CHURCHWARDEN
OF THIS PARISH
1971–1980
PER ARDUA AD ASTRA
ALSO HIS BELOVED WIFE
MARGARET MARIE
1918–1985

They lived at Nailards. We find in the parish magazine for September, 1981: 'Any parishioners who might be apprehensive about propping up their umbrellas in their usual place may feel rest assured [*sic*] that Brian would have had no wish to interfere with an old established custom.' An even older custom was to dip your fingers in the water stoup, which would probably have been inside an earlier porch on the right side. It is with your right hand that you make the sign of the cross.

*   *   *

I have seen visitors passing through the door, this south door of the church, and not stop to look at it. What of greater beauty do they anticipate finding inside? In the Decorated style, it is a fourteenth-century addition, the most elaborate thing in Amberley. And yet it achieves lightness: the concentric mouldings around the pointed arch are as slender as they are numerous. I would like them to be painted in bright colours, each different, like a student's scarf. Sustaining them are clustered shafts, two on either side, with capitals whose leaves of oak and vine are deeply undercut.

Is the rôle of this door to prepare us for the interior? It is undoubtedly a fine overture, one you tap your feet to, but it has little in common with the opera we shall shortly be hearing. Not, however, because it was composed last: most overtures are composed last; only the break is usually less than a hundred years or so. By then a new style had evolved, one in which Nature, if not exactly deified, was cherished as God's handicraft. This svelte door belongs rather to the churchyard, which is not without leaves of its own: ivy that man has planted, nettles that he poisons. So I was mistaken in using the word 'overture': what we are seeing is rather the culmination of what has gone before. This is not Art the hand-maiden of Architecture so much as Art the sister of Nature. And observe how the trunk of the yew, with her clustered shafts, provides the perfect link.

The porch having tended to flood when heavy rain fell, a drain was dug in front of it during the winter of 1905/6, and a grating placed over it. But this clearly sufficed not, for in the parish magazine of August, 1938, we read:

> Our first object is to make a waterproof channel all along the base of the Nave walls, and to clear all the pipes. How necessary this work is will be realized when we state that there was at least one opening in the walls of the South Aisle below the surface, through which quantities of water have been soaking underneath the floor of the Church for a long time past. It is not surprising that green mould is to be seen upon the southern support of the Chancel arch and elsewhere in the South Aisle, and that the Church has been cold and damp in the winter.' This was precisely the area in which murals would subsequently be discovered.

To the left of the porch is another two-light window, but it is in the style of the fifteenth century, Perpendicular. Renewed in 1965, not necessarily for the first time, it almost replicates what went before, as is confirmed by a photograph of 1910.

In the west wall of the aisle there is a lancet of the same ample proportions as the one in the east. To the left of it there is a pilaster strip, similar to the pair on the north side. It buttresses the arcade that replaced the south wall of the Anglo-Norman nave.

In the south side of the tower, no less high than the aisle roof, is a little lancet that once lighted the way to the belfry. It is now filled with nine knapped flints. But in 1895, descending to within a metre from the ground, a bigger lancet was created. Not very tall, but certainly broad, its purpose was to light the new vestry on the ground floor of the tower.

There is a west door, Early English in origin. Its six planks are

Victorian replacements, with nails to hold the ten-plank inner layer, which is older by far, even perhaps original. The surround of the arch, again Victorian, consists of a double hollow chamfer beneath a hood moulding with label stops.

Interior

Amberley Church, despite asymmetry, is axial. Which point of the compass does it face, though? Early Roman basilicas have their altars in the west, but St Augustine of Canterbury, sent to England by St Gregory in 597, insisted on the orientation that we have come to deem obligatory. And we may wonder why the letters 'N', 'S', 'E' and 'W' need adorn the weathervane, for they tell us what we were already justified in assuming. Indeed our instinct, surely, would be to check the letters by the church rather than the other way round.

The nave is not without a secondary axis, a transverse one, from south to north. 'Axis' may be an exaggeration. And yet, ere we stepped inside the church, something of the kind had unfolded: it began at the façade of the porch, which is Victorian gothic; it proceeds to the south door, which is Decorated. On opening this, we encounter the central bay of an arcade: it is Early English; and the vista culminates in a round-headed window, set in the former north doorway, which, you will remember, is Anglo-Norman. Thus, as the eye progresses from arch to arch, it reaches ever further back in time.

A track of seven centuries! But time is not what truly impresses us: it is space, rather. Space that fans upwards. Dare one speak of a crescendo from cabin to cathedral? Forget that: a guidebook is hardly the place for hyperbole; or for alliteration either. Enough to say that here is no ordinary interior. I am not, of course, suggesting that St Michael's,

Amberley, is a second St Botolph's, Boston, vast, unified, flooded with light from every angle. Not at all. But we feel no less of an expansion within. The impact is just subtler, and therefore perhaps all the deeper.

Turn and look at the door surround: as on the outside, there are multiple mouldings, but they form a kind of rere-arch to the equilateral arch of the doorway. And behold, outside the porch, that yew. She has stationed herself a little to one side so as not to block the vista.

Now turn again. What was I saying a moment ago about the interior? A fanning out, or something. How low the south wall of the aisle is, how high the north wall of the nave! – a contrast that is emphasized by the discrepancy between the windows, between journeyman gothic and sophisticated Anglo-Norman.

Something similar is happening over our heads: the timbers of the south aisle tend on the whole to be a cut below the ones on the original nave. Do not misunderstand me: whether of the aisle or of the body, they are all demonstrably kindred – cousins german. But those up there – this is Amberley talk – are town. These down here have more difficulty in keeping straight, so accustomed are they to our lanes. And both lots at such proximity! Well, a wall tactfully segregates them, the wall of the arcade. It also, one has to say, obstructs our view of the nave-roof when we are in the aisle, and of the aisle-roof when we are in the nave. But if we position ourselves beneath one or other of the arcade's three pointed arches, we become fully conscious of what is stretching over our heads: the underside of the great diagonal that dominates the exterior. Happily no stone vault has subsequently dignified it out of recognition. And, for whatever reason – conservatism perhaps, or, more likely, lack of funds – the fifteenth century did nothing more than enlarge one window. No clerestory: the timbers continue to occupy their original position, in ancient simplicity. Even the loftier ones, town cousins though they may be, refrain from lording it. There is not an

Interior of Amberley Church, Sussex, 1820

angel of the meanest rank to corbel them, let alone Michael himself.

When the rafters deteriorated to the extent that they could have fragmented and fallen, they were covered in match-boarding. This was only removed in 1960, when they were largely replaced. In December of that year the parish magazine reported:

> Many of you will have seen some of the timbers which have come out of the Chancel Roof – one of them fell out when it was touched! . . . at times there is a terrible mess, but we must be thankful that we have such devoted and careful workmen, who clean up on Saturdays. This inconvenience will not last for long and it is hoped that the scaffolding will be out by Christmas.

You may remember my hinting at a south-north axis. Well, I am beginning to doubt whether I have convinced you it actually exists. But what of that other axis, running from west to east, which we know to be the principal one? It has been thrown off-centre by the addition of aisle and porch. And the south door, the normal one of entry, is at the furthest point from it. There are, sure enough, all those east-facing benches, which, if we lose our bearings, can give us some idea of the direction in which the high altar should stand; but as for its specific whereabouts, what clue have we? As yet, only a north-western sliver of chancel. True, the floor of the nave rises towards the east, but you never noticed this, did you? It may not even have been the wish of those who laid it that you should: they knew that a level floor created the illusion of a downward-sloping one, so perhaps they just wanted to counteract this. But whether obviously as at Idsworth or imperceptibly as at Amberley, seldom did the mediaeval builders fail to create what George Herbert in *The Church-floore* called

> The gentle rising, which on either hand
> Leads to the Quire above.

The south aisle, needless to say, has its own axis: it runs parallel with the main one. At its west end there is a lancet, obviously restored by the Victorians, who, I suspect, also widened it and heightened it. Of clear glass, it most happily gives onto a pair of openings in the curtain wall of the castle. These too are lancets. And lancets, wherever they may be situated, speak of church – which may explain why the aisle, though bantam, punches above its weight.

Did I say 'lancets'? But we know the curtain wall of the castle was not built until 1379. They cannot therefore derive from the Early English era. In actual fact they were introduced in 1908. At that time the owner was the Duke of Norfolk, who decided to repair the walls: we read that they were in a parlous state.

Kindly turn about. Beneath the splay of the east lancet is a deal altar of 1865, purely utilitarian, and perhaps a touch shameful for a place of worship. A cloth and frontal, however, cloak its modesty. Nor could anyone find fault with its scale, which is so apt that you would vouch for its being site-specific. In reality, however, it started life in the chancel, whence it was moved in 1967. This is another way of saying that the aisle – for the first time since *c.*1550 – became a chapel again.

Our assumption that the aisle was originally a chapel is confirmed by the presence of a piscina near the east end of the south wall. Though it is just a rectangular niche with a single drain, no one during its centuries of disuse has had the heart to do away with it, so snugly does it pillow itself in the angle of a roll-mounding, which, bar one break, extends at knee height from the south door. A half-metre away from the south-east corner, or even slightly less, it climbs before continuing along the east wall, where it runs immediately below the window splay. It thus clears the altar. At the same time it says 'sanctuary'. Oh yes, there is something special about this area, for no matter how tiny it may be, it is where death and resurrection are enacted, no less than in that bigger space beyond the choir stalls.

Interior

To the east of the south door, beneath a rere-arch, is a pair of lancets. Originally there was another pair to the west of the door, but this was enlarged to become the window we know today. It is in the Perpendicular style, which developed from Decorated in the late fourteenth century and eventually became Tudor. Very late gothic, it differs markedly from the Early English openings on the left and the right of it, not to mention the Anglo-Norman ones opposite. It has cinquefoils, which are seen nowhere else in the church, only simulations of them in stained glass. By Amberley standards, one has to say, it is rather elaborately crowned. And yet, in its reduction of Gothic to the basic rectangle, it left the pulpit window, which is two hundred years its junior, little further to go. We might even say that it is domestic in feel. It has a sill. And with only 75 cm separating it from the floor, it is at coffee-table level. Mugs, indeed, have been known to rest on it. There is also a certain domesticity about the wall itself, which is the church's thinnest – logically enough, being the most dwarfish. And it seems even thinner than it actually is, at least in the vicinity of this window, whose glass, unlike that in all the others (which so keeps its distance that it is wellnigh flush with the exterior) comes forward to meet us.

Beneath the window there is an inscription. It commemorates the Michells, a couple who lived at The Leith. In the left-hand half of the slanting surround is written: 'In memory of HELEN BEATRICE MICHELL. Died 31 May 1963.' In the right-hand: 'Air Raid Warden London 1940–45 Guide Commissioner Arundel 1954–58'. Across the vertical surface below, just above the sill: 'and KENNETH MICHELL. Died 25 December 1967. Aged 80'. He too could say, 'I have done the state some service.' A commander in the Royal Navy, he was awarded the DSC, and, in a subsequent business career, the OBE. The lettering *re* the wife is by Joseph Cribb (1872–1967), Eric Gill's first pupil; *re* the husband by one of Cribb's own pupils, Kenneth Eager.

*   *   *

I have already referred to the old photograph of this perpendicularized window. From it we learn that the leadlines have been altered somewhat: they were previously all lattice-work, but now we find floreate curves from the top saddle-bar upwards. Are they the lilies of the Blessed Virgin Mary? The south aisle was originally the Lady Chapel, and they may be intended as a reminder of this. Obviously twentieth-century, doubtless dating from the reparation of 1965, they harmonize with the old-style cinquefoils, which themselves have a botanical air, taking the name of a plant whose leaves terminate in five leaflets.

This window was so enlarged from the original pair of lancets – indeed it reaches as high as the eave – that in 1965 there was concern that it might collapse. Hence the extra layer of stone beneath its segmental arch. This is obviously new, for it so cuts into the spandrels that we are left with a square peg in a round hole – if not a quart of milk in a pint jug.

Of all the windows that could have been substantially enlarged, why this one? Why not the one on the other side of the porch, for it is near the altar, upon which extra light could fittingly have been bestowed? Instead, an area to which we attach no special significance has been thus favoured because it is where the font formerly stood. And of all the seven sacraments the one most associated with light is baptism: candidates forsake the darkness of the world to be illumined by Jesus, the *Lux Mundi*.

> 'Christ is here, all is light,
> Shadows of the past are gone.'

Nor did this symbolism have to wait for the enlargement of windows in the late gothic period, for it goes back to the first millennium: in the compilation of the Romano-German pontifical (tenth century) the giving of the lighted candle was added to the christening service.

Interior

Since the south aisle is an addition, the font cannot have been there from the start: it was in the nave, and freestanding, so that the baptismal party might gather round it, representing the universal Church in the dish of the world. It would not have been all that far from the west door, in those days an external one, at the opposite end from the more spiritually charged east; for baptism is the first step.

The shift of the font to the south aisle, in front of the perpendicularized window, must have been welcomed by all but the most hidebound; for there it was better lit, without being any further from the west end – and so master of its own space that one might almost have spoken of a baptistry. Admittedly it was far from any door. But then, if it had stayed in its original position it would hardly have been any closer: the addition of the tower meant that the west door of the nave was no longer an external one.

On the evidence of a Regency watercolour the arcade was blocked, doubtless to make a school of the south aisle, so the font was again moved – to the west side of the west pier. As far west as before, indeed. If not farther. But it was less well lit. And no longer freestanding.

The early Victorians were not prepared to countenance the perversion of God's House to the teaching of the three Rs, so the partition was removed. Clarkson founded a new school, at his own expense, in Oak Tree House. The Clarkson Room. Why then was the font not restored to its previous place in front of the perpendicularized window? Because, for the first time, congregational seating was installed in the south aisle. That was in 1864, and in the same year the font was shifted for the third time, suffering damage in the process, to the west side of the *east* pier.

And there, alas, it still stands. Oh, I can conjure up a defence – if I must. Where better than the nearest convenient spot to the south door, which by 1864 was the only one in normal use? The idea of baptism as entry (who can doubt?) had endured. But why has the font forsaken the west? Well, this is not so odd: with the passing of the Middle Ages, orientation has counted for little: Santa Maria della Salute stretches south-north, the Brompton Oratory north-south. Let me add, nay stress, that neither of these two churches rejects orientation in the liturgical sense: if the sun omits to shine and you are without your compass, you will detect nothing unusual. Quite otherwise are those churches whose lines converge on the centre And what about the symbolism of light? Does that no longer count either? Unless we leave the door open, no other place in the whole of St Michael's is darker.

Well, so what? Since 1935, when electricity replaced our oil lamps, daylight has mattered less. But no invention will ever compensate for the worst drawback of all: our font that was designed to be free-standing, as all fonts are, is no longer so. Well, one day it will be again. Five benches in the western half of the south aisle were removed to make way for a choirwomen's vestry, but now that the whole choir, both male and female, vest on the ground floor of the tower, the area in front of the perpendicularized window is again vacant. The font needs it. It needs the font.

*   *   *

Nothing in St Michael's is older than its font. Twelfth-century, probably coeval with the church itself, it provides a beginner's guide to Romanesque architecture, the prime shapes of which are the circle and the square. The bowl, chipped at one angle and unrestored, is a parallelepiped. From it a hemisphere has been gouged, and what is that but a round-headed arch, inverted and rotated through 360°? Around the outside runs a blind arcade, each of its four sides being carved in low relief to represent four Romanesque openings. These, all of which approximate to a double square surmounted by a semicircle, are no less geometric – and hardly less basic – than the bowl itself. But we may wonder how they could come within the twelfth century's limit of tolerance, liberal though it was, for they are far from identical. I have to say that in Pulborough, where we again encounter a font of this Anglo-Norman pattern, the blind arcading admits of no such discrepancy between arch and arch. Was our own craftsman a tiro, then? Or did he do the job on Saturday afternoon? It matters not, for we find the rubato to out taste.

The bowl rests on a polyped which dates from the reparation of 1864: it consists of five cylinders, *i.e.*, a massive central stem and, contrastingly slender, four corner shafts of Purbeck marble. The latter have replaced wooden colonnettes, whose capitals and plinths were like round cushions, Cretan in simplicity. Equally Victorian is the base. This, like the bowl, is square, but comparatively elaborate in that it rises in two chamfered tiers. Of these the lower one lacks a sliver on its east side, having been joined to the base of the adjoining pier. Herein is precise asymmetry, the contrary of the bowl's rough symmetry. Roughness we warm to, and symmetry we recognize as indispensable to an object that should stand at the centre of the baptismal party.

What was that about the font at the centre of the baptismal party? Some hope. And as for its east side, this, one has to say, is almost completely obscured. Deprived of the opportunity to express its purpose, it could be a side-table on which to stand a vase of flowers. Wait for the next wedding.

The font cover is round and of oak, with a raised, *patée forme* cross. It has a circular centre, around whose thickness is written in gothic lettering – black, except for the capitals, which are red: 'The Thank Offering of Mothers 1898.' The gratitude is for having given birth and for the churching that followed.

*   *   *

Raise your eyes from the font's blind arcading to the actual arcade that divides the body of the nave from the south aisle. What a difference between pointed arches and round-headed ones! On the other hand the two cylindrical pier-shafts, though Early English, could be Romanesque; nor is there anything of your gothic uplift about the moulded capitals. And the bases? They have inherited the circle and the square – a round cushion on a parallelepiped. On the other hand those four spurs, now worn, which stretch to the corners of the latter, are all thrust, like pointed arches, like the tower's diagonal buttresses.

Though round-headed arches convey no such thrust to the eye, they nonetheless exert an outward pressure. Try aligning a pier of the arcade with the responds of the chancel arch and you will observe that the northern one leans outwards, for it lacks the southern one's abutment, namely a wider stretch of wall to which, eventually, the south aisle was added. Indeed the whole north wall of the nave leans outwards, as is clear at any time your attention is drawn to it, but especially at night when the nave is lit and the chancel is in darkness.

And so? One side leans, the other not. That may sound visually disconcerting. But quite the contrary: your eyes, if they are anything like mine, will enjoy the northward tug, which conspires to counterbalance *die Sehnsucht nach dem Süden*, to which extension after extension has succumbed. This tug, despite adding a further asymmetrical element, puts all its weight into symmetry's restitution; for the north wall still remembers the old days when it had a south one to answer it. Each of the two original windows on the north side had its southern twin, as did the north doorway. No arch in the entire nave that was not rounded. Or in the chancel either.

Let us revert to the present: although the west door of the nave and the window above it have retained their central position in the wall, the former has been gothicized, while the latter, the original one, is no longer external. Instead, being twice as wide as the other Anglo-Norman windows, it allows us ample sight of the lancet in the west wall of the tower. Furthermore (to summarize what we already know) the north wall of the nave has acquired a rectangular window; the south wall has been largely replaced by an Early English arcade; every window in the chancel is now a lancet.

Can we say homogeneity has largely given way to mishmash, symmetry to lopsidedness? Before we answer that question we must again conjure up the church in its original state. Given the central position of the west window, we may deduce that the south wall of the Anglo-Norman nave was exactly where the arcade is now. Nor would we expect anything else, given the gothic penchant for recycling. Even the piers themselves may be the remains of wall. It follows from this that our church can at no stage have been completely symmetrical: there was always a greater extent of wall to the south of the chancel arch than to the north. This, of course, allowed room for that nave altar. Not only in Gothic, therefore, did symmetry cede to function: we may add with practical certainty that the apex of the nave roof, though directly above the west window, has always been to the south of the centre of the chancel arch.

Basic Romanesque architecture is the solid geometry of space and the proportional arrangement of parts. Thus Amberley's twelfth-century nave was as broad as the walls were high, and twice as long, while the chancel was a square that culminated in a semicircle.

The present plan is virtually the opposite: the addition of the south aisle has transformed a long nave into one that is roughly square; and the chancel, once short, has grown long.

At least, however, both the Anglo-Norman soffits have survived: the northern one is external and unchanged, the southern one runs along the south side of the arcade, sustained by five beam-ends, from which the roof of the south aisle begins its downward slope.

The Anglo-Norman openings are closely related to each other, the insides of the windows being similar to the outsides of the doors, and vice versa. Yes, 'doors': the plural is no misprint, they include (a) a south one, which must have existed until the addition of the south aisle, and (b) the chancel arch, which is a door of sorts, but *sui generis* in that it has never had an external side proper. External in a sense, however, is the west side, in that the nave is more exoteric than the chancel. That is why the zigzags, added *c.*1160, do not extend to the east side.

We have already seen that the outside of the north door has a roll moulding and must originally have had nook-shafts. We can only guess what its capitals were like.

Capitals with palmettes and nook-shafts, intact, flank the insides of the windows.

Similar, albeit grander and more complex, are both the north and south sides of the chancel arch, with its palmette and volute capitals, zigzag carving, and, instead of nook-shafts, half-columns, three on either side. The windows' outsides are comparatively plain. So too, I would imagine, was the inside of the north door, now blocked and at one with the wall, except for the window in its top third, a stilted, round-headed arch. Its interior splay is quite plain. The splay of the easternmost Anglo-Norman window is uncomfortably crowded by that of the pulpit window, but its stone surround has been plastered over, thereby alleviating the situation somewhat.

This fenestral ectopia would disturb us more if the church's various cells were symmetrical, but none of them are. Not even the chancel: true, its north and south walls both lean outwards, having no abutment except the clasping buttresses, and only those since 1864. But it stretches 15 cm further towards the south. This is much less than the nave ever has, but still noticeable, if only because the choir stalls, when seen through the chancel arch, protrude more on the left.

The church's greatest access of asymmetry arrived with the south aisle, which is asymmetrical even in itself: its roof slopes one way only. This gives it a somewhat jaunty air, which would appear to be infectious: the six purlins angulate their way along at alternately higher and lower levels, and the easternmost is much the shortest, thereby allowing for a principal rafter from which a lamp or pyx could hang above the mini-sanctuary.

These rafters have definitely decided to dress down: despite the altar, they look as if they were doing a day's work in a barn rather than attending divine service. Quite frankly, they come over as a little too meagre for the job in hand, despite a principal one for every three subordinate. Sensing this, they have summoned help from two braces, but of the roughest and readiest. Propped against the capitals of the arcade's two piers, they look like a temporary solution that only time has sanctified.

On the other hand, this come-as-you-are south aisle – all the more casual for having no north one to balance it – is consistently gothic. And for the most part genuine. The west respond even has an original carved head to grace the finial of its chamfer.

Although the north door, as seen from the outside, and the Anglo-Norman windows, as seen from the inside, are more grandiose than we have any right to expect of a village church, they are as nothing compared with the chancel arch. This, the church's chief feature, looks exactly as it does in an engraving that appeared in *Excursions through Sussex* (1820), by William Deeble from a drawing by Thomas Higham (17954–1844), so it can owe hardly anything to Victorian reparation. Authentically Romanesque, it is almost Roman-imperial in majesty. What, though, if its columns are engaged? No fewer than three on either side, they can afford to be. As such, they themselves make for elaboration; but it is the elaboration of massive simplicity, only possible on the thickest of walls.

Amberley Church

Let your eyes travel round one respond or the other, starting at the semicircle of the half-column that extends furthest into the archway; then let them continue along the straight surface, no matter whether eastwards or westwards, make a right-angle turn, work their way round another (but smaller) semicircle, straighten out again and finally make another right-angle turn, this time into a stretch of wall. At journey's end, what has it amounted to, this sequence of half-columns that alternate with corners? A lesson in geometry? One day, when no one is looking, I shall paint a horizontal line round these responds, north red, south blue, and thereby dispense with anything so cumbersome and lumbersome as words, with their temporal drag. At a stroke I shall have explained to you how our Romanesque builder, Euclid having been rediscovered, played with the circles and squares on which his aesthetic depended.

Circles and squares. The capitals too, allowing for variations on the theme, are each a circle that metamorphoses into an square, in this case an annulet into an abacus. Similarly the moulded bases are a fantasia on the circle; and the slabs on which they rest are rectangular, though the symmetry of those on the north side has unfortunately been jostled by the first two steps of the present pulpit. So I suggest that the respond on which you should concentrate is the south one.

Glance back at the piers of the arcade: imagine them upside-down, and, lo and behold, you will discover that they are an Early English variant on the half-columns of the chancel arch.

*   *   *

The responds of the chancel arch, remember, have half-columns that come in threes. Moreover, the arch itself is in effect three: a central one; a second that oversails it; and a third that oversails the second, only more so. A rainbow in shape. Perhaps originally a rainbow in colour.

The receding right-angle between the middle and outer of these three arches – three in one – is prolonged downwards by the right-angles (here they are outward thrusting) between the half-columns of the imposts. There is thus one continuous line that not even the capitals interrupt – provided you stand at an angle of 45°! And the rest of the lines? No matter where you stand, they fail to match up, but only by a few centimetres, not enough to prevent the whole mighty arch from achieving unity.

Or at least it did in *c.*1103, when it was new. But some half-century later, the Anglo-Normans having reached full maturity, it was treated to those zigzags and chevrons. The inner arch, including the introdos, and the outer one, including the soffit, were carved with zigzags, and the middle one with upward-pointing chevrons. The latter's soffit, however, was left bare for some reason, perhaps because it is the narrowest.

All this is the mechanical carving of your semi-skilled mason. Mechanical but not machine-like. The zigzags vary in width, as do the voussoirs into which they have been cut. Such inaccuracy we have already met on the font. It existed because it was tolerated, whereas we moderns, suffering from a surfeit of machinery, go further: we regard it as a plus, contrasting it with the lifeless precision of neo-Romanesque. Not that Ian Nairn (1930–83) is uncritical, even so: in the 'Sussex' volume of *Buildings of England* he complains that the chancel arch, which he prizes, is 'spoilt by a tragic difference in scale of the detail.' Happily he finds the triple responds 'huge and forceful'. But wait for it: 'huge' too are the capitals that 'support a three-order arch which alas is full of finicky zigzag ornament, almost embroidery, even on the soffit. The effect is as incongruous as Adam trying to imitate Vanburgh.' Writing under the general editorship of Sir Nikolaus Pevsner, whose formative years coincided with the Bauhaus, he accepted as an article of faith that *veritas* was architecture's corner-stone: buildings, being static, should appear so. To convey movement were to lie. Well, may columns not soar? Most certainly, even the half-columns of our chancel arch. But observe the great arch that links them: it is a pledge of eternal equilibrium. Except that some twelfth-century Robert Adam has come along and added all those zigzags, as restless as the word itself.

Would I wish them away, then? No no. Indeed, I want them to continue down to the floor. But, since they do not, I ask myself whether a greater unity might not be achieved if I were to climb a ladder, file in hand, and obliterate them. Occasionally I do – in the mind's eye. Or, if imagination fails, I turn to the Anglo-Norman windows for comparison.

Alternatively I enter the chancel, walk up to the sanctuary rail, and, on turning round, look in vain for any of the arch's zigzags, bar a foreshortened sliver on the introdos. Nothing jives; our Ian Nairns would say nothing jars: from this angle we observe the architecture of sobriety, the only visible sculpture being two small heads on the responds' middle-of-three capitals. The southern one wears the Spanish beard before it was invented. However, it had no intention of playing the hidalgo: it simply occupies the V-shaped cleft between two palmettes. The head on the other side may once have been very similar, but is too worn to be read. *N.B:* Neither of them is visible to the congregation. They are themselves worshippers: they face eastwards, altarwards, as does the one in the south aisle. Such heads we find on Carolingian buildings, descendants of pagan ones.

Whatever carvings of the human form may once have peopled Amberley Church, there are no other survivors, unless we include eight triglyphs: like that bearded head and its companion, they nestle between palmettes – on the same two capitals. Now, it is on a frieze that we expect to find triglyphs, but ours – oops! – have slipped. Moreover, they point downwards, like that Spanish beard. And for precisely the same reason. In calling them 'triglyphs' I am simply tracing them to their putative source. In fact they are hands – with three fingers, the middle one being the longest. By far.

Eight hands. Except that one on the south side must have disappeared, and the restorer who filled the gap made no attempt to reproduce it.

If the mediaeval stonemason had confined himself to carving one hand only, I would confidently say, 'This is God.' Now, church-crawler that you are, you expect to see the Ancient of Days as an old man, 'His garment white as snow and the hair of His head like the pure wool'. Here, however, He takes the older form of the *Manus Dei*. And if He has only three fingers? That makes sense, whether because the dip between the palmettes allows no room for more, or because the Father is one with Christ and Paraclete. But eight of Him? I have to admit that they may have been intended as no more than a decorative motif, one that is repeated at regular intervals, like triglyphs on a classical frieze.

In triglyphs, I dare say, the mediaeval mason read the trinitarian number, which dictates the form of the arch itself. We encounter it again in the three-bay arcade, the three-times-three windows of the chancel, and two windows and a door in both the south side of the aisle, and, originally, in the north wall of the nave. But are we in very truth looking at a theological symbol? Maybe at no more than a phoneme in the masons' language of décor.

*   *   *

The Victorians, who tended to treat parish churches as miniature cathedrals, not infrequently built up the chancel floor to a higher level than that of the nave. At Amberley, however, they can have been put to no such trouble, for the print of 1820 reveals that there were then, as now, two chancel steps, only they were not where they are today. The lower step is (and has been since the reparation of 1864) in line with the east wall of the nave, the upper one with the west wall of the chancel. They are as wide apart, that is to say, as the chancel arch is thick. Standing between them, in the centuries before there was a pulpit, the preacher preached – as indeed our incumbent at the time of writing does, unless there is a full house, for like his Master he dispenses with notes. At the time when the print was made, however, the upper step was where the lower one is now, and the lower one was at some distance to the west of it. We may therefore justly speak of there having been nothing narrower than a dais, or what the early Church called a *bema,* on which deacons placed a table in time for communion, removing it afterwards. And that is what our Georgian sidesmen did. Thus, for some time, Amberley had a kind of nave sanctuary, a successor to the one at the east end, which was simply abandoned.

This transformation the print has faithfully represented. No altar in sight. Instead the focus was on the pulpit – not the present one or its immediate predecessor but a two-decker with sounding-board. It projected well beyond the north side in order that the congregation, occupying box-pews not only in the nave but also in what we would call the choir, might see and hear the parson.

And the sanctuary? It counted not. Although there was an altar rail, it had no altar to rail: of plain wood, stretching from the north wall to the south, it simply reinforced what the steps had come to say: 'Thus far and no farther.' And certainly the reverend gentleman would have had difficulty in projecting his voice that far: sound, as acoustical tests have verified, travels better from the chancel to the nave than vice versa. And as if to reinforce this practical consideration, the balusters were as simple as the rail. Thus we can date them to the eighteenth century, no earlier. Those from the time of William Laud, Archbishop of Canterbury (1633–45), or of Charles II (1660–85), when the altar was roughly in the position that it again occupies today, *i.e.,* either at or near the east end, would have been turned, even if quite modestly, as at Southease, rather than magnificently, as in the chapel of Petworth House.

*　　*　　*

The interior of the east end falls short of perfection. The central lancet, which, if anything, should have more headroom than those on either side, has less: all three are framed by identical curtain arches which rise to within centimetres of a horizontal beam. But, despite this, they succeed in making their combined statement, particularly as they once again have stained glass: they constitute an alternative to a reredos. *I.e.,* they bear witness to the altar which stood immediately below them, until it was moved forward, so that the priest might celebrate *versus populum.* This is unfortunate, but a worse thing can happen – and has.

The orientation of an axial church is so inherently climactic that anyone who sets his heart on making semantic nonsense of it need only remove the high altar from the sanctuary and install it in the nave. The focal point of the perspective is thereby reduced to bathos, as indeed is the entire chancel. Amberley, it is true, originally had a nave altar, but, unlike the Georgian communion table, it stood to one side, against the wall immediately to the south of the chancel arch. It thus left no one in any doubt as to its subaltern rôle: it was quite literally a 'side altar'.

In the later Middle Ages the special holiness of chancels was emphasized by a tall screen, in most cases wooden. Not many have survived intact, though more here than in other Western European countries. The one at Amberley lost its pierced upper part during the Reformation or the Commonwealth, but its solid lower part, two metres high, was still there in 1864. We may marvel that the Georgians should have tolerated even this remnant, which by coincidence has rather an early Christian look about it, but they valued it for non-sacerdotal reasons: the clergy had ceased to officiate anywhere except in the pulpit and at the font, but the chancel continued to accommodate a hierarchy of sorts, for here it was that the chief families sat – in pews they paid for. In 1864, immediately prior to the great reparation, Clarkson and his churchwardens certified to the Incorporated Church Building Society, at 7 Whitehall, that 'they found twenty-six sittings, in the Chancel, appropriated to the Vicarage and two farm houses, held under lease from the lessee or lessees of the Lord Bishop of Chichester, and the whole remaining portion of the said Church free and subject to allotment by the Wardens, according to Law, according to the best of their judgment.' Thus the elect, enjoying semi-privacy, could look down on the under-parishioners in the nave.

This was a travesty at which Laud would have blanched, but, *mutatis mutandis*, there was a precedent, for though some lords of the manor, as at Amberley, were clerical, most were lay; and yet in the Middle Ages they and their families had had a place in the chancel. This may have had its origin in the Saxon manorial set-up, the retainers occupying the hall and the thane an adjacent chamber, separated by a partition with a central doorway. In the two-cell churches they must have felt truly at home.

*　　*　　*

A nave from which the chancel was semi-detached; from which the south aisle was sealed off entirely; and – for evidence we have that print of 1820 – from which all sight of the roof was barred by a flat ceiling: it only just cleared the beam above the chancel arch.

A nave? A drawing-room, more like.

I mean no misprision: churches have always borne a resemblance to the more fashionable domestic interiors of the day, differing only to the extent that evening dress differs from day wear. Thus St Michael's in the twelfth century, with its small, high windows in large expanses of wall, could have been mistaken for an Anglo-Norman keep. The thirteenth-century additions went some way towards turning it into the hall of a Plantagenet baron, which is to say it became lighter, though it was still virtually unfurnished, except for a ledge round the walls to accommodate the old and inform, like the bench-table we still find in cloisters.

Then someone made comfort a fetish; and someone else, around the same time, invented long sermons. So pews were installed.

And at home nothing but a chair would do.

When palaces acquired musicians' gallery, so did churches.

In 1837 Queen Victoria came to the throne. The Oxford Movement and the Cambridge Camden Society dismissed the Georgian dilettante, who had found the Middle Ages barbarous, as a barbarian himself: churches ceased to look like drawing-rooms and were made to look like churches again, complete with neogothic fittings. Meantime the rich were building themselves villas that aspired to a similar aesthetic.

*   *   *

Light can create shadows; light can obliterate them. In 1820 the walls of the nave, not excluding the wooden beam over the chancel arch, were whitewashed. Nonetheless, in the print of that date they are dark, being in deep shade, all the deeper for one patch of sunlight. This sunlight should have emphasized whatever was spiritually significant, should it not? Instead, barely reaching the pulpit, it floods some box-pews, of all things – not, I hasten to add, because our artist slavishly copied the chiaroscuro that he saw: his sunlight comes from the direction of the great diagonal roof, which is windowless! Nevertheless, it both creates the kind of pattern we find in drawings by

Soane, and helps describe the objects on which it falls. And have we not said that light was a symbol of the divine? Yes, but if only it were less fragmentary! The phenomenal world, the great outside, is more liberally illuminated.

Now let us see how our printmaker has treated the chancel. What Larkin called 'the holier part' is light throughout, in the days before electrics an impossibility unless it were charged with supernatural radiance. Well, at least the roof-beams are dark, being of wood, and no Georgian has whitewashed them. Why trouble? They are remote from the main action, which centred on the pulpit in the nave. But observe what our printmaker has done to them: he has left their undersides unshaded. He is thereby informing us that the light came from below. Can it be that the high altar, though demolished, continued to emit a power, like the missing megaliths of Avebury?

This is not so much the light of the Neoplatonists that descends from on high as the *claritas* of St Thomas Aquinas which rises from below, from the intimacy of things, a manifestation of the organizing form, *consequens formam substantialem solis.* The early sun shines through the chancel's east windows, but, despite that, or because of it, the chancel itself is solar.

Except chronologically, the word 'Georgian', as we understand it, ill suits our printmaker, who was a romantic – a neo-mediaevalist, if you will. In him the rationalist aesthetic was under threat, as was rationalist theology. He imagined a space that the next generation would restore to us – directional, teleological, reaching towards the transcendental.

*　　*　　*

With the arrival of Perpendicular, if not before, Early English space, one way or another, was under threat, but never from people who were totally hostile to Gothic – until Georgian man: he considered it at best quaint. What did he do, then? He transformed our nave, which is where the action was, into a shoebox.

And now? What is there to show for this *illuminato*'s pains? *Niente!* All that he achieved, all that he stood for, has suffered reversal. You feel sorry for him? Dry your tears. One day the mediaevalists will again be worsted. In 1935, quick to follow French and German precedents, Roman Catholics built the Church of the First Martyrs, Bradford, with a central altar. 'Bravo, begad!' said the ghost of the Georgian. The reply was grudging: 'We can see, dear ancestor, which way you were heading, but you never quite got there. It was up to us to eliminate the last vestiges of hierarchism, whether sacerdotal (the tall pulpit) or secular (the rich-poor divide). God is equality.'

Meantime at Amberley we have scarcely budged. But our children will. Do I mean that the high altar, already brought 1.65 m forward from the east wall of the chancel, will again find itself in the nave? No no. That were again to make nonsense of what the edifice is saying, and yet fall short of the modern ideal, which is communal informality. There exists only one solution: pull the intractable place down and start again. The new St Michael's, called Amberley Mitsubishi Meeting Room, will look much like home, or like that home from home, a place of entertainment, for home itself has become a place of entertainment. And it will point to itself, saying how innovatory it is, oblivious of the fact that it is adhering to the most ancient of ecclesiastical traditions.

*   *   *

Though, in 1864, Clarkson restored the chancel steps to the positions they had occupied in the Middle Ages, he was not so single-mindedly antiquarian as to overlook the exigencies of current liturgical practice. Thus, aware though he was that mediaeval sanctuaries tended to be a mere pace (allowing room for altar and celebrant, but little besides), he retained the far ampler one that we have come to consider normal – post-mediaeval though it is, probably dating back no further than the Laudian reforms. Laud generally insisted that the sanctuary should stretch all the way from the north wall to the south, thereby allowing for a more adequate length of altar rail at which the faithful could kneel to receive communion.

In Norman times, we may be sure, our altar was freestanding, situated on the chord of the apse, but in the extended chancel it stood against the east wall. The probability is that it was of stone: wood, though common in the early centuries of Christianity, was exceptional in gothic times. But, regardless of the material, the place of sacrifice was accorded wellnigh celestial status: Laud at his trial called it 'the greatest place of God's residence upon earth.' Some ecclesiologists even say that churches were made for altars, not altars for churches, but this is a pious exaggeration: unlike Greek temples, churches are 'about' people. The Quakers refer to their 'meeting house' which translates '*ecclesia*', the Latinization of a word that the Athenians used for a regularly convoked assembly of citizens. Even so, we may affirm without fear of argument that Christians have generally liked their high altars to be high indeed; that is to say, set in a raised area.

Well, the altar at Amberley is raised, is it not? – the sanctuary being two gradins higher than the choir. But that is scarcely going to satisfy our mediaeval ancestors: 'Raised, yes,' they may allow, 'but not in the altar's immediate vicinity.' I want to get this straight. 'Is that tantamount to saying it's on the level?' They do not even trouble to reply. Instead they just point to the roll moulding, which runs round the chancel walls, immediately below the window splays, rising at right-angles when it is little more than a metre from the north-east and south-east corners. It then reverts to the horizontal and continues at the same level beneath the higher windows in the east end. It has taken no notice of the rise in the floor at approximately half the distance from chancel arch to east end, for the Middle Ages had long been dead when the sanctuary was so amplified. But it informs us where the altar rose from its single close-hugging step.

Or maybe *two* steps: a higher one that was no more than a pathlet (wide enough for the celebrant to cense his way round the three free-standing sides) and a lower one, stretching to its entire width. This is what was discovered at Tutbury Castle in the 1980s when the ruins of St Peter's Chapel were excavated.

*   *   *

Under the east window, fixed to the wall, are a pair of wrought-iron sconces, whose drip pans have frilled edges. They date from 1909.

*   *   *

There are an aumbry and a piscina in the north and south walls respectively, both doubtless original to the extension of 1230. If they appear to be set too low for adult use, that is because the sanctuary has been extended as far as the wall below them: the floor was raised by 33 cm at a time when neither the aumbry nor the piscina was in use. Originally they were at the same height from the floor as the piscina in the south aisle.

In mediaeval times the aumbry, in the absence of a vestry – the priest vested at the altar – may have simply been a cupboard for storing candles, vessels, vestments or liturgical books. The word 'aumbry' is related to the old French 'almarie', a variant of 'armarie' (modern 'armoire'), which derives from the Latin 'armarium', a closet or chest, a place for 'arma', utensils. This would account for its remarkable simplicity, the only refinement being sides whose edges are chamfered and terminate in finials. That is to say, it is no less plain that the piscina. The usual practice, in England at least, was to reserve the Host in a pyx, but that does not rule out the possibility that the aumbry served this purpose, too: in the collegiate church of St Julien de Tours, as we happen to know, a viaticum was kept in the aumbry, while the Blessed Sacrament for the canons was administered from a *suspensio* (pyx).

Whatever the uses to which our aumbry was put in the Middle Ages, since 2001 it has contained a ciborium, given to us by the Confraternity of the Blessed Sacrament. Its curtains, of the four alternating seasonal colours, were made by Edna Cable. It needed a white light, and the question arose, 'What sort?' The Diocesan Advisory Committee having opposed an 'off-the-peg' brass fitting, the Reverend Stephen Guise, our incumbent at the time, suggested that Andrew Breese, of the blacksmith's shop in the Amberley Working Museum, should design one. He chose to reflect those candle brackets on the east wall of the chancel. A brass wall-plaque says:

THE AUMBRY WAS BLESSED
BY THE RIGHT REVEREND CHRISTOPHER C. LUXMOORE
(ASSISTANT BISHOP DIOCESE OF CHICHESTER)
CHRISTMASTIDE 30TH DECEMBER 2001
THE LIGHT WAS GIVEN IN THE MEMORY OF
S[HIRLEY] JOHN GUISE

Here, let me explain, is an appropriateness and a link: John Guise was a metalwork teacher and the grandfather of Stephen, who donated both light and plaque. Stephen also donated, in memory of his Aunt Prudence, a ciborium that is used on Sundays for the distribution of the Host. At other times it is kept in a safe.

It was at the suggestion of Stephen, whose fault is to think better of people than they deserve, that I embarked on this book.

Inside the Tower and on the Top of it

The public are not admitted inside the tower, so I shall be brief. The low squat lancet in the south wall was inserted in 1898 to the design of P. E. S. Streatfield, and is 'similar in detail to that in the west wall of the south aisle.' It lights the vestry, which was created by the construction of a ceiling. There has since been a ringing gallery on the first floor, at the level of the lancet in the west wall. Access to it is by wooden stairs on the north side. There is also an Anglo-Norman window in the east wall which affords a bird's-eye view of the church. Through this the Georgian choir, having climbed a staircase or ladder, stepped on to the gallery that was affixed to the west end of the nave. An aluminium ladder (this is very boring) rises up the south wall and gives access to the intermediate chamber. A wooden pole-ladder, on the same side, has twenty-five rungs and a pitch of 24 cm, leading thence to the belfry. The bells hang level with sound openings on all four sides, the sills of which are approximately halfway up the bell-frame.

* * *

We possess a ring of five bells in the key of B. They are among the lightest in Sussex and unusual in that they are rung anticlockwise. They were cast in the parish of St Andrew's, Holborn, and transported by cart to Amberley. The founder was Robert Catlin. The inscriptions read:

1 Prosperity to the parish of Amberley. R Catline fecit 1742
2 R Catlin fecit 1742
3 Robert Catlin cast & hung us all 1742

4   The Revd. Mr Bell Carleton, Vicar. R Catlin fecit 1742
5   Daniel Newell Robert Harmes Church Wardens R Catlin
      fecit 1742

The view from the top of the tower, though precipitous, rewards the climb. To the west you see over the curtain wall of the castle. To the north you will be surprised how blue the village pond has become. To the east is thatch of combed wheat, the original of Ellsworth Kelly's shaped canvases. To the south is a map of the churchyard, 'peopled with the spectral dead'. Beyond it rise the Downs, which Cardinal Manning declared to be 'only less beautiful than Heaven'.

Decorative Elements

Like almost all of Europe's old churches, ours has lost its mediaeval treasures and most of its decorative elements. In compensation there are some modern ones, the great majority dating from the first third of the twentieth century.

The temptation of the mediaeval Christian was triumphalism. And that of the modern? Secularism. St Michael's has resisted both. The church that the Anglo-Normans built, though not without some aspiration to grandeur, is far from vainglorious: the Early English chancel is long but simple; the tower sturdy but not disproportionate; the south aisle unforgetful of its subaltern rôle. Nothing really contradicts the defining Christian virtue, humility. You will look round the walls in vain for any boast of heraldry. We have not a hatchment to our name. True, the Wantele brass includes arms on the tabard, but it was laid in the floor for people to tread on – an objective correlative for the word *humilis*. With the passing of the Middle Ages one might expect to find Baroque *schwulst*, but there is only the faintest trace of it; and no neo-Roman glorification of Empire, of its soldiers and administrators. Nor are there any of those Tommies with the half-incredulous look that they wear on finding themselves in khaki glass: the Roll of Honour honours them more worthily. No corner of this public church has become someone's private chapel. No weepers weep. The few souls that have been memorialized were mainly vicars, and these, even the most scholarly, have put aside their Hebrew, Greek and Latin, being content with English – plain English at that, as plain as the stone in which it is incised. Admittedly our stained-glass windows borrow the courtliness of the late Middle Ages, even of the High Renaissance, but they have been placed at the service of religion: there is no vignette of Amberley, complete with a Calcott, biplane, artist's easel and such stuff. And the surviving murals are commensurate with the space they adorn.

THE MURALS

Our murals fall into two main categories, pictures and writing, the former pre-Reformation, the latter post-. None of them are so legible as they once were. Observe that I expand the word 'legible' to include both types. The pictorial ones are verbal in so far as they tell stories. The verbal ones, moreover, are artistic in so far as they are calligraphic; but, unlike the pictorial ones, they tell no stories: they express abstract ideas. Indeed they are themselves abstract – abstract art as opposed to the figurative and story-telling kind, hence viewed with no disfavour by the iconoclast – though that Renaissance wit, Sir Thomas More, would tease us by saying that words are themselves images.

There is also some foliated decoration, which, as it teaches nothing, may strike your missionary heart as frivolous. You will quote St Gregory or Luther, who commended the image as a teaching- aid. And so it may be. But what about the topmost roundels in the windows of

Canterbury Cathedral? You can decipher even these, did you say? Then you must be up a ladder, or have mastered the art of levitation. I congratulate you, but please realize that individual scenes matter less than the total abstraction. Rudyard Kipling took the trouble to tell Rider Haggard, 'Colour, old man, is what, *au fond*, clinches a creed. Colour and the light of God behind it.' Hurrah, my Ruddy boy, just so! To enter a church is ideally to be afforded an inchoation of life in the presence of God's throne. And as the Celestial City cannot be divided against itself, no matter how many its ballarats, so unity of design, diverse though its components may be, is the first essential. This the early Catholic understood. The first Puritan did too, and I would beseech you, dear friend, to stop calling him a Vandal. I abhor this racialist term, especially if applied to someone who substituted clear glass for stained, who covered frescoes with whitewash, and who removed statues that in his view muddied the purity of line and plane: he had different taste, that is all – minimalist rather than maximalist. Distancing himself from Abbot Suger, he formed a fellowship with Bernard of Clairvaux, in whose saintly eyes images were a distraction from worship: '*superfluitates*' he called them. Admittedly neither you nor I would stoop to giving aesthetic innovations a theological spin, but never let us praise or blame a work of art on account of its *style*, for that were the gravest of heresies, a truly burning offence. Say after me, then:

O! what a power hath white simplicity!

All right, all right, you will force me to admit that I would rather Amberley Church had remained as it was in the Middle Ages. I would indeed. But that has little to do with art, even less with religion, and a lot with antiquarianism.

It is we moderns, who, careless of the whole and its oneness, have lost the essential spirit of our ancestors. A hubbub has replaced the choral sweep, and this has become so pervasive that we no longer take it for what it is, an aberration. As the English Augustan satirists never ceased to remind their own contemporaries, the abnormal is in danger of becoming the norm. Thus the new Coventry Cathedral (1951), which abuts the ruins of the old, was designed as a space you wander around, looking at things. Its antecedent is not Ste Chapelle but St Michael's, where one individual donor after another has suited his own taste.

*   *   *

In 1967 Mrs Eve Baker, ARCA, restored, nay, largely brought back to light, our surviving murals. In 1864 most of the internal plaster had been chipped away, and with it much painting. But certain areas escaped, all of them in the nave and aisle, chief of which is a set of seven panels, stretching the entire width of wall between the respond of the chancel arch and the arcade. Here, mercifully, is no flint and rubble but ashlar, to which paint, over the finest cream ground, could be directly applied. The surviving colours are little more than red ochre in the panels and yellow ochre in the border. There were also likely to have been charcoal black and lime white, which, when mixed, make grey-blue.

Circular and vertical lines have been scored into the stone. These, I think, belong to a decorative scheme that dates from the twelfth century. But not the painted mural, as some people suppose. It can be no earlier than the south aisle.

Look at the Crucified: He is surely pierced with three nails, not four, *i.e.*, only one for both feet, otherwise His right knee would not be so bent. Though three-nail Crucifixions already existed by the twelfth century, they were of Cathar invention, hence, unsurprisingly, reviled by Rome as blasphemous – until she adopted them herself. Does this volte-face brings a smile to your lips, gentle reader? Well, I must ask you to understand that in the long run it is artists, not theologians, who determine iconography. Orthogonal Romanesque adhered to the *Christus triumphans*, arms horizontal, the rest vertical: He stood, as it were, on His own two feet. But Gothic, with its aesthetic of ascent, was happier when burgeoning from a point, as those leadlines in the top of our perpendicularized window, though only dating from 1965, eloquently tell us.

There is no point in hypothesizing that our mural was the work of Catharans, for it cannot in any circumstances be twelfth-century – not if I am right in thinking that the wall on which it is painted contained an Anglo-Norman window. This I believe to have been blocked when it was shifted to become part of the new south aisle. Allowing for a mural. But within a century and a half this fell from grace, for it expressed nothing of the late mediaeval, early humanist mood. The bourgeoisie was growing in power and numbers. All classes were becoming richer, including the lowest, at least after the Black Death. When choir screens became the rage, Amberley felt no qualms about building one, even if it encroached on our mural. For what did those seven panels say to Chaucer's merry pilgrims? Christ's Passion, Resurrection, Majesty? They said a primitive style of painting, a primitive life-style. No landscape of abundance. No landscape at all. No ornament. Of ultramarine or lapis lazuli not a grain, only colours dug out of the ground at your feet. Well, we've moved on, good sir. You like this Gascon wine? It was a good year, 1367. Let me top you up.

The screen must have had a staircase, or why should those two rectangles of no paint be so far from the archway? The corner of one of them cuts into the Saviour's face, but that is unlikely to have been a cause for concern: the mural was largely obscured in any case. What about finishing the job with two good coats of whitewash, and spare the Reformer his pains?

Only the destruction of the altar may momentarily have pricked a conscience or two, but a new one could be installed on the rood loft. Failing that, there had long been the south aisle with a perfectly good altar of its own.

In the fourteenth century modern man wanted the good life. And yet, if you will allow me a moment's sermonizing, the Good Life, with capital 'G' and 'L', is precisely what those *passé* panels are all about. Do the arms of the suffering Christ hang, or are they raised in an all-embracing gesture, glad of the *sige-beam* , as the Old English poet called it: the victory tree. The cross is life-enhancing, and so it has always been, or, if not always, certainly long before Good Friday came along – in the East with the swastika, in Egypt with the ankh or ansa. And I trust that the mediaeval vicars of Amberley, while celebrating in the nave, drew strength from this image of descent-ascent, of their paradoxical God who was Himself the sacrifice: it depicts not only capital punishment at a moment in history but a daily death that is itself resurrection. They called it the mass.

When those distant predecessors of our present incumbent, whose names are known to us from 1370, stood at the altar, their eyes were approximately level with the head of Christ.

Christ has two figures on one side, two on the other, so you would be forgiven for supposing that He was at the panel's centre. Actually He is a little to the left. Above on three levels there are six more scenes, each divided vertically down the middle.

Did I say 'middle'? No, here again the division is fractionally left of centre, in line with Christ. At every level there is more to the right than to the left. Well, what do you expect? This is Amberley Church, after all. No matter where you look, this lurch towards the Downs! *Die Sehnsucht nach dem Süden.*

The mural has a border, predominantly yellow, depicting, dolphins, whales or such like, but now faded. What meaning does it have? Perhaps none except to divert, as in illuminated manuscripts, or to express the Creator's fecundity. But fish, it may not be irrelevant to add, can allude to the feeding of the five thousand, which in turn symbolizes the eucharist, as do Christ's post-Resurrection appearances.

Along the top there runs a cornice, which is simply the extension of an abacus of the chancel arch – frame enough without need of a painted border. A painted border, though, runs down the left side in a straight line. The one on the right is of equal length, but it shifts sideways and back again, like those purlins in the south aisle – to the left, thereby accommodating the impost of the arcade's respond, then, at the spring of the arch, back to the right, and further.

And a border divides the four top scenes. 'See how it makes a cross,' I say. 'How could it not?' you reply. And you add: 'Don't try and tell me that the symbol of Christianity was hereby specifically intended.' 'Wait a minute,' I insist, being determined not to let you get away with this; 'cast your eyes down to the tier immediately below. This too depicts one scene on the left and another on the right, but there is no border down the middle. How do you explain its absence? Answer me *that*.'

Below these five panels, containing six scenes, stretches that *Crucifixion*. I say 'stretches' because it covers the mural's entire width. Though no formal device sets it apart from the rest, it is clearly special, and not simply on account of its size: it has been plucked from its chronological position in what is otherwise a processional sequence from bottom to top. It is out of sequence because it is out of time, *for all time*, and placed lowest – 'on the line', as the Royal Academy would have it – nearest to where the altar was: it is the altarpiece, no less.

Unlike the other panels, which are approximately square, this is approximately the shape of two squares side by side, like the plan of the Anglo-Norman nave. Why so long? Long it needed to be: besides Christ on His cross, there are the two thieves on theirs, set lower, of course.

And the thieves themselves are distinguishable from one another: the good one on the dexter turns towards Christ, while the bad one on the sinister faces the viewer. (The two angels in the east windows do the same. Nor is their symbolism entirely unrelated. But that is sheer coincidence: at the time when they were made, our mural had not yet been uncovered.) The good thief's head is upright, and so is the bad one's, judging by bodily posture, whereas Christ's inclines – but only slightly, enough to say that He, unlike them, is already dead. Arms bent at the elbows, the body sinks. But, dear reader, be so good as to trace the lines of it from feet to hands: they rise. They are more alive than those of the living thieves, who are simply not-yet-dead, whereas He is The Life. Those outstretched arms say, 'Come unto me.'

Between Christ and the thieves are the Blessed Virgin Mary on the dexter, St John the Evangelist on the sinister.

*   *   *

Above the Crucifixion, on the left, is the Flagellation. A micro-cephalous Christ, wearing a knee-length garment, his hands tied in front of him, is bound to a stake that would have been too slender for the purpose, very likely, were He not the very image of motionless rectitude. Slender Himself, He contrasts with the scourgers on either side, whose heads are so large that you would take them for masks. And from masks they could well derive, the kind worn in miracle plays that priests and others performed inside the church. Contrasting with Christ, these henchmen are grotesque. No such caricatures are to be seen in France, and even by English standards they are extreme, though the Emperor Maximinus has been treated with comparable indignity at Little Missenden: no Roman in real life was ever like him, except, in some measure, Vespasian, who helped himself to Sussex.

If I can hardly begrudge our muralist his travesty, it is because I see herein a certain poetic justice: there was nothing that Roman artists liked more than to depict their fellow-countrymen as beautiful, the barbarians as ugly. When you see the contrast between Christ and His scourgers, greater than that between Him and those thieves who were crucified on either side of Him, maybe you deplore that those menials should be so travestied. 'After all,' you say, 'they were only obeying orders.' Gentle reader, this painting you misinterpret: its butt is the congregation. 'Ye remember *Dorian Gray*,' it says, 'so don't tell me ye're comely without: ye're ugly within, and Christ's true flagellation is your own evil-doing, not what those Romans did unto Him. Ah, what was that ye said? Heathens too can sin. Yea, and how! But not *before* God. It is ye, not they, who are at His side, scourge in hand.'

*   *   *

Ugly brutes! How those scourgers contrast with the Man-God! As different as Hell from Heaven! But they are only ugly in so far as they depart from our ideal of the human form. As shapes on a plane, Christ and they are equal in beauty.

And of equal legibility, even from a distance. That applies to all this painter's forms, including the cross on which no perspective has played its illusory tricks. Having lost detail, they are little more than silhouettes. That, in essence, is what they always were. And the essence survives, amen.

In the accompanying scene to the right we re-encounter the same three characters, but the two Romans, or ones very like them, are now on the left and in the middle, Christ being on the right: He is on His way up *Gûlgûltâ*, Golgotha – Calvary, that is to say: the place of a skull. I name that precious hill polyglottously in the hope of wearying you, if I have not done so already. May you tokenly feel the climb's strain, for our mural will fail you there. Correction: the ascent must be telling on that Roman with a hammer and his mate. How heavy they are, so fat-headedly heavy! How will they be able to goad their crucified man Calvarywards? Answer: they will not need to. Rather their job is to keep up with Him. How light He is, light-hearted, this Light of the World! And no long garment obscures the lissomness of His south-pointing stride. Look: He is about to career out of the picture frame!

Not a bad Friday, then – a good one in fact. As for His cross, that instrument of torture, death and victory, He makes nothing of it, it is as unburdensome as a lance: He is the young knight, eager for tilt or fray. Do you smell fear on Him? No, this is nothing but a hike, an excursion to the top of the Downs, *die Sehnsucht nach dem Süden.*

Here, reader, is the spirit of the first millennium, before Christian art took the byroad of human anecdotalism. It is Byzantium, plus the movement of Gothic.

*   *   *

A little girl at the village school, having been taught the Sermon on the Mount, assumed that the mount in question was Amberley. In her, I declare, lie the makings of a mediaeval muralist. Had she in fact been one, I hope she would have had the spirit of ours, whose Bible, in every scene he touches, is one of good news – you miserable sinners.

*   *   *

Though, as we have said, there is a chronological progression (excluding the altarpiece) from bottom to top, there is none between left and right. Instead, those on the left have been reserved for scenes with fewer figures. That is why the painter has drawn the vertical divide a little to the left of centre.

At the next level we have the Resurrection on the left. Christ, cross in hand, steps from His tomb, below which, in arches, are two sleeping soldiers, one with a lance.

On the right is what everyone assumes to be a post-Resurrection appearance. We see the heads and shoulders of five figures, but little more: much has been lost to one of the blocks that held the staircase.

At the top level on the left is Christ in Majesty. Between his feet is a globe with the cross imposed. He holds his hands at shoulder height. This is the *orans* posture that we see in pre-Christian religions; and in the catacombs – not to mention our central east window.

On the right the risen Christ, cross in hand, appears to Peter.

*   *   *

In the south aisle, on the side of the east respond of the arcade, there is some branch-work painting. And Clarkson writes in *Notes on Amberley* : 'Our Saviour, with the *nimbus*, sitting on the lap of the Virgin Mary, crowned, with an ecclesiastic below, is on the eastern wall of the aisle. Purer and sounder teaching from the Word of God is developed on the right and left of the foregoing, almost the whole of the 3rd verse of *Revelations* ix being visible, and some portion of *Hebrews*, x.23. There appears to be some sub-work of a Pre-Reformation date.' (The former text is given incorrectly: it should be *Revelation* iii. 19. To miss it on account of a typographical error could be costly: 'As many as I love, I rebuke and chasten: be zealous therefore, and repent.')

What Clarkson called 'sub-work' has emerged as the seven-panel mural since the restoration of 1967, when the superimposed text from *Hebrews* was removed. The text from *Revelation*, to the right of the side altar, has partially survived. The *Madonna and Child* is now a blank wall to the left of the south aisle's east window. In 1865 it was the church's most prominent mural.

On the south wall, to the left of the door, is a beautiful fragment of

Decorative Elements

The Visitation: on the left is the head of the Blessed Virgin Mary, on the right, touching it, that of Elizabeth. In *Notes on Amberley* (1865) Clarkson tells us that 'a pleasing effect is realised by a few simple lines.' He goes on: 'A continuous curve serves for the eyebrows of two faces.' Mrs Baker reports: ' Two female heads, one with nimbus, but I would say that these have been so much repainted that it is doubtful whether anything original remains.' Judging from Clarkson's description, the repainting must have occurred between 1865 and 1967. The style of the Virgin's head is fourteenth-century. Of Elizabeth's, unfortunately, little remains.

These murals confirm, surely, that the south aisle was a Lady Chapel.

* * *

Two red consecration crosses survive, one on the north wall of the nave, the other on the west. We learn from Clarkson: 'Two, on the west side of the south door, one higher than the other, were obliterated in 1864. Another was to be traced on the pier at the S.W. of the nave.'

Originally there are likely to have been twelve consecration crosses on the interior walls and perhaps another twelve on the plastered exterior ones.

THE WANTELE BRASS

(On the return wall of the arcade's east respond)

This brass was originally laid in the pavement of the south aisle, near the altar. It was removed in 1864 to its present setting, where it is backed by a slab of Sussex marble. The inscription reads: '*Hic jacet Johannes Wantele qui obiit xxix. Die Januariii, Anno Domini m.cccc.xxiv.,cujus animae propitietur Deus.*' (Here lies John Wantele who died on 29th January 1424, on whose soul may God have mercy.) If you refer to the illustration you will see that the Latin is actually abbreviated but I have written it out in full.

Amberley Church

Sir John lies bare-headed, clean-shaven, his ungloved hands conjoined in prayer. He wears plate armour from which a mail shirt protrudes about his neck. Over his pointed sabatons are rowel spurs. The Reverend E. Noel Staines, Vicar of Amberley, 1961–70, writes in *Dear Amberley*: ' . . . The brass is unique as the figure has an emblazoned surcoat over the armour. It was originally enamelled and the red, green and silver colours were visible in the nineteenth century.' Or, as the Reverend George Arthur Clarkson had written, a hundred years earlier, 'Wantley's tabard bears, Vert, three lions' heads, langued Argent.' But he went on: 'There is authority for supposing that the brass was not enamelled, but that some resinous or other soft substance was introduced for embellishment.' This only confirms my disbelief that the colours can have been either enamel or original. If they had been, no one, surely, would have allowed them to be rubbed away during the course of the twentieth century, at the beginning of which they were still visible. I am inclined to suppose that they were a romantic addition, probably dating from the Regency. The internet comes up with a drawing of the brass which must date from around then. It is coloured to perfection, showing no wear, which leads me to suppose that it is the work of a craftsman who was after a commission to embellish hitherto unpainted metal.

*   *   *

It is as well never to forget that this brass was made to lie horizontally. It so happens that the lion at Sir John's feet reads better vertically, but it is a rest, not something to stand on. Nor need we marvel how his sword stays upright without anything to grip it!

Near the south door there is a reproduction of this brass, horizontal, as the original once was, but at table height, convenient for rubbers.

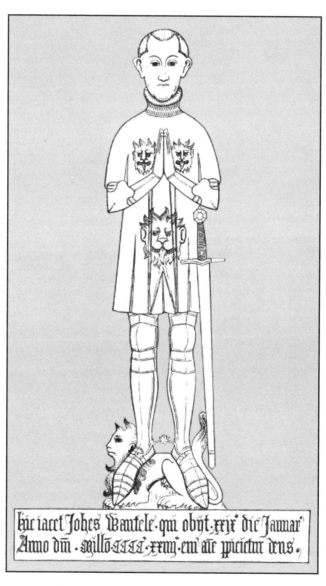

The monumental brass of John Wantlele,
Amberley Church, Sussex. 1424

Decorative Elements

STAINED GLASS

The windows are most unlikely to have had stained glass before the thirteenth century. Would they previously have been open to the elements, then? Not on the evidence of Pumpton Church, where Anglo-Norman paintings on a splay are in an excellent state. Protection may have been provided by horn, some bleached fabric or wooden shutters.

The supreme artistic achievement of the Middle Ages, as far as North-West Europe is concerned, was stained glass. Though there has been a revival of it, dating from the second third of the nineteenth century, there is no art form against which post-mediaeval man has shown such hostility. Much has been lost to sheer neglect, but the spirit of the Enlightenment was most to blame: in the eighteenth century the Canons of Notre Dame ordered the destruction of most of its windows, and even Chartres suffered somewhat from a bishop of similarly enlightened views. It was probably the English Reformation, an enlightenment *avant la lettre*, that denuded Amberley, leaving nowt to Puritan zeal. At any rate, we have not a single window whose glass is mediaeval, or even a part of one, and the fragments that were discovered behind the wall to the south of the chancel arch were too small to justify their reinsertion. But even if an entire set had survived intact, we would not be seeing them as they were in the thirteenth century, for they would be islands in a sea of whitewash, whereas in their day they were just one element in a decorative complex that included murals and decorated roof timbers. Not even stone was considered finished until it had received a lick of paint. And this, augmented by much finery, was all in the service of ritual, ritual in the service of God. By the fifteenth century, however, the *gesamtkunstwerk* began to suffer demolition: stained glass was contributed by individuals as fancy took them, picturing figures of their name-saints for the most part, or their coats of arms. An instance of this may have been provided by the perpendicularized window in our south aisle. Vanity of vanities, it may have been inscribed with the name of the donor, as in St Mary's Church, St Neots, Huntingdonshire, but not that of the person memorialized. Stained glass from the first third of the twentieth century has come to fill half our windows, replacing clear glass and lattice-work, which survive in the other half.

Disparate though our stained-glass windows may be in style and subject-matter, they have one (albeit negative) quality in common: they depict a world in which no one does evil, not even Satan himself, who is simply being worsted. And did I catch you saying that they were more realistic than our murals?

The Clarkson Windows

(The three lancets in the east wall of the chancel)

These three windows, which ask to be read as a triptych, contain Amberley Church's first stained glass of modern times. Across the bottommost level, distinct from the figuration, is written:

> To the glory of God and in ✧ memory of Rev G. A. Clarkson ✧
> Vicar 1840–1897 ✠

To us he is the man who was responsible for the reparation of 1864, but this merits no direct mention in his obituary, which appeared in the inaugural number of the parish magazine, for January, 1898:

> . . . Appointed to his charge in 1840, he only quitted it at the call of his Master in 1897. This means that he lived in one country cure all through the great church movements, the results of which we are now feeling . . . He built a room at his own cost, long before national education was thought of, and himself a scholar of repute at Cambridge, determined that Amberley should be provided with

the means of instruction . . . As years rolled on and fresh ideas sprung up, he was ever ready to give them a trial in his parish, and all those aids to social and mental development in village life, whether from a distinctly spiritual side, such as the Mothers' Guild, or the more secular, as the County Council Lectures, found from him a ready welcome . . . '

Having been Rustat Scholar at Jesus College and 47th Wrangler, Clarkson, himself a clerk, was ordained deacon in 1839 and priest in 1840, the year in which he was appointed Vicar of Amberley with Houghton Chapelry. He was the author of *Notes on Amberley* (Sussex Archaeological Collection, Vol. xvii, 1865), *The Appellate Peers and the Crucial Rubrics* (1878) and *Lychgate Notes* (1881).

Clarkson was further memorialized by a brass desk, whose whereabouts are unknown. As it was to stand beside the altar, there can have been no justifiable objection to its being inscribed with one of the three sacred languages. As we learn from the parish magazine for January 1900, it was 'specially suitable for a memorial of one who . . . was not only a most kindly gentleman, but a scholar.' Scholarship is indeed required: besides Latin, one must know what the initials stand for:

A.M.D.G. & I.P.M.
Rev. G.A.CLARKSON, VICAR,
MDCCCXL–XCVII

Here it is in full: '*Ad majorem Dei gloriam et in piam memoriam.*'
Our brass collection plate is embossed with a circle of leaves that terminate in three leaflets, and, on the underside, this inscription: 'D.D. Rev G. A. Clarkson VICAR JUNE 4TH 1868 ON THE OCCASION OF HIS MARRIAGE'. 'D.D.' stands for '*Deo dedit.*'

*   *   *

By the time that Picasso was painting *The Barefoot Girl* some parishioners may have believed that an incumbent who was born in the reign of George III had too much of the past about him. I wonder, though, how much of a new broom his successor was. The Reverend William Champion Streatfeild, to his credit, founded the parish magazine. (How did we ever exist without it?) And in the issue for July, 1898, we read, 'On Whit Sunday the choir wore cassocks and surplices for the first time.' In January, 1901, he urged parents to stop their children smoking, which 'hinders the growth of both body and mind'. Well, let us salute the reverend sir as our coeval! At the time, however, he may have seemed out of touch with the new century. And in *A Vicarage Family* Miss Noel Streatfeild tells us how necessary Sunday clothes were when her father was vicar: ' . . . everybody, absolutely everybody, had to have them, even if they were returned to the pawn shop on Monday morning.' He went on to become Vicar of Eastbourne and finally Bishop of Lewes.

Nor would it appear that our next vicar, the Reverend George Frederick Carr, LLD, was one to stand nonsense. In the parish magazine for February 1905 we read:

> The Churchwardens wish the following to be inserted: – "I, George Baker, humbly apologise for wilfully and deliberately disturbing the congregation of Amberley Parish Church on Sunday evening, January 8th, and I promise, if legal proceedings are not taken, to conduct myself in future in an orderly and reverent manner in the House of God. [Signed] Geo. Baker."
>
> This is the first, and we sincerely trust the last, time we shall have to refer to a matter of this kind in our Magazine. It is, of course, the duty of the Churchwardens to see that order and decorum is maintained in the Church and Churchyard before and after, as well as during Divine Service . . .

And it may be well to mention here that loitering in the Church-yard or Church Porch is expressly forbidden.

No loitering! Is this ancient severity? No, modern! Look at the loitering that went on in Clarkson's day, if our cover sketch is trustworthy. On the other hand Carr rode a motorbike. We know this because in October, 1910, he thanked most gratefully his parishioners for their kind enquiries and sympathy with him whilst laid up in consequence of skidding on a hill.

*   *   *

Clarkson can hardly not have known the almost equally long-serving vicar of Burpham, where there is a window to pay him tribute. The inscription reads: 'Giving thanks to God for the honoured memory and faithful ministrations of Robert Foster 48 years Parish Priest of Burpham his parishioners and friends dedicate this window AD 1899.' His parishioners and friends had wasted no time, clearly, for it dates from the year of his death. Perhaps the tardier people of Amberley were spurred by this example. At any rate, in the number of our parish magazine for May, 1901, we read:

It is proposed to fill the three windows of the Chancel of Amberley Church with stained glass, picturing our Lord's Ascension, in memory of the late Vicar, Rev. G. A. Clarkson, at a total cost of £80. Mrs. Clarkson originally offered, at a cost of about £40, to do the middle window only, but she has most kindly acceded to the Vicar's wishes and given £50 instead towards the cost of three windows. The work will be carried out by Mr. E. J. Prest, of Haverstock Hill, London . . . The Vicar proposes as soon as this can be done to issue some Subscription lists, and meanwhile will be very glad to receive any contributions, however small, towards this great addition to the beauty of the Church, which Mr. Clarkson loved so well, restored at a very great cost, and held as Vicar for the wonderful period of 57 years.

Mr E. J. Prest, I should explain, was the manager of the firm of craftsmen who made the glass. The designer was 'our friend Mr Lane'. At 4 p.m. on October 10th, 1901, the windows were dedicated by the Archdeacon of Chichester, the Venerable E. L. Elwes. The Reverend L. Newman played the cornet. All expenses having been paid, there was a surplus of £2. This was spent on a silver-plated flagon, thus completing the vessels used at Holy Communion.

Though the Clarkson Windows are set in the culminating wall of this axial church, they detain few visitors. That is a pity, for they are consummately planned, and mean well. Set in lancets, which are the simplest of pointed-arch surrounds, they simulate contrastingly elaborate niches. The Victorians, with their tendency to 'gild refined gold and paint the lily', not to mention their cult of naturalism, were happy to remind us that Early English was not the whole of Gothic.

* * *

In the central window we see Christ ascending. In the left-hand one an attendant angel, wearing golden shoes, is looking inwards, *i.e.*, towards Christ; and in the right-hand one, another angel, wearing light green ones, looks straight ahead. The subject suits the situation, first because lancets themselves are a kind of ascension, secondly because the east is the direction of the rising sun. Thus orientation, which the Georgians had wanted to minimize, was protracted by the Victorians, reaching, as was always implied, to Jesus beyond: '*Eum cujus nomen est Oriens*', as John Donne says on his monument in St Paul's.

* * *

Set as they are in fictive niches, the figures ask to be read as statues. Statues? But they are brightly coloured! Well, gothic ones were, too.

A beauty of these three windows is that they relate to the celebrant at the altar, who, like the ascending Christ, stands with his hands raised to shoulder height, while the angels' vestments are the model for his or her own.

A famous precedent for the angelic priest, or priestly angel, appears in the Portinari Triptych, by Hugo van der Goes. Perhaps 'our friend Mr Lane', who designed the windows, was attracted to this iconographic rarity by way of allusion to his firm's name, 'E. J. Prest' (priest). The glass is otherwise unsigned.

Did you say you have yet to see any of our vicars in golden shoes, or in pale green ones either? Spiritually they wear both pairs – simultaneously: the angel in the golden ones is turning his head inwards towards Christ, the one in light green is looking straight ahead – at us. Gold is the colour of the eternal world, pale green of Amberley. These attendants, with their undifferentiated features, represent the dual aspect of our vicar, who officiates beneath them.

I would venture, in strictest confidence, to add a further gloss for your benign consideration, that these angels are our churchwardens: on the left is the vicar's warden, looking inwards at the priest, on the right the people's warden, looking at the congregation.

*   *   *

I say that Christ is 'ascending' rather than 'ascended' because He is standing, not enthroned. Along the scrolls borne by the angels is written: 'Lift up your head O ye gates / The King of Glory shall come in.' (*Psalm* xxiv, 7) And across the bases of their niches stretch banderoles, on which is written: 'So may we also in heart and mind thither / ascend and with Him continually dwell.' (From the collect for Ascension Day)

We have seen how artists nearly always draw Amberley Church from the east-south-east, the most informative angle. Similarly, in the central window, Mr Lane has chosen the most informative moment of the Ascension: Earth is implied by a grey cloud, Heaven by the rays that fill the background, for a mandorla has shoe-horned itself into this tall, narrow space.

It is quite usual for golden mandorlas, which are emblematic of light, to be held by an angel on either side. (The convention derives from sculpture.) Angels we have, but, being in separate windows, they are too far away to render such a service. Instead they carry scrolls, and this may seem less menial. On the other hand their distance renders Christ more central and unique: like Melchizedeck, He is not only the Great High Priest but King too, as confirmed by the border of crowns – an old device: we see examples in the Victoria and Albert Museum, X09389 and X09390.

*   *   *

Late gothic windows that culminated in tracery bred stained-glass canopies to fill the interstices. What fantasy these allowed the designer! How ironical that ours, who, filling simple lancets, had no such excuse, should have chosen this device, and even taken it to an extreme! Well, the Victorians liked excess. They also liked naturalism, and they found more of it in late Gothic than in early. Also the single figure per light. This chimed with their statue-mania, and a statue must perforce be implied by a figure in a niche.

A statue, one only. Therein lies the problem: a single figure sufficed not to fill a space so tall and narrow as an Early English lancet: Mr Lane's solution was to make fictive niches whose canopies and bases were egregiously tall and whose sides were egregiously narrow.

Then there was the little matter of iconography. There could be no *Christ in Majesty*, as in the Clayton mural, or even in our own, for a seated figure would suit the space even less. But an Ascension? Where would the eleven remaining apostles go, even in this broadest of the three lancets? They are represented by the cloud that received Jesus out of their sight. And on it He is standing as if it were a base like those of the statuettes that surround our pulpit. A boss in Norwich Cathedral shows God the Father on such a base, though a glory of light surrounds Him. The angels on either side of Jesus are standing, too; and He, like them, occupies a niche, between spindly, banded pillars, which are set diagonally, like the mullion of our pulpit window. We might therefore argue that He is as much a statue as they are, but our eyes say 'no' to this. Unlike the angels, whose feet are firmly planted on their plinths, He is in the sky, on that cloud. Well, why should 'that cloud' not be stone, painted grey? Similarly the background of golden rays could be stone that is gilded. But this is not what we expect of a niche, so He is likely to register as a figure in a landscape, or rather in a Heavenscape, the Living Lord, more exalted than the angels on either side of Him, who, by contrast, are set lapideously in the wall of Amberley Church. Or am I exaggerating the difference? They too, after all, are set against sky – not, however, a golden Heaven, but the deep blue of night, though with golden stars. Let me add that this was such a conventional way of decorating a convex ceiling that no one, surely, would interpret it as the infinite dome above.

(Forgive me) I have just been testing you: there are in fact no golden stars; there is no night sky. Instead there are golden flowerets against a ground of deep blue leaves. And they recur in the openings at the base of the central lancet's fictive niche. But would you have known this unless I had told you? I call them golden stars in a night sky because normal perscrutation tells you so: only by pressing your nose against them would you be able to confirm what I have just told you. And they have no smell.

The fact that the central lancet is only slightly higher than the side ones creates a design problem, for Christ is *much* higher than the angels. True, His plinth is larger, prominently inscribed in gold with

'IHS', an abbreviation of the Greek *Iesous*, or (take your choice) the initials of the Latin '*Jesus hominum Salvator*' – though I draw the line at '*Jesus habemus socium*' – whereas those of the angels are crossed with a mere banderole of black lettering; and though all three wear haloes, Christ's is coloured and cruciferous (a privilege exclusive to the Persons of the Trinity), in strong contrast to the angels', which are plain white. On the other hand Christ's canopy, though broader than those of the angels, is vertically challenged. This was unavoidable. By way of damage limitation, Mr Lane has made it more plastic than those on either side. Here, we feel, is glass simulating stone as such, whereas the angels' canopies are so two-dimensional that glass seems to be simulating stone that is itself simulating lace. More importantly, the gulf between Him and them is conveyed in physiological terms: Christ is tall, with ascetic features. He could scarcely be anyone else: that 'IHS' at His feet is more honorific than informative. We might better have been told the names of the two angels, but they are so anonymous as to be indistinguishable: both are relatively short and stocky, they have largish heads, and, like all except the most exalted specimens of their species, are chubby-cheeked.

Angels? You are left cold by them, admit it. But maybe this was intended: the theology is Christocentric, Christ being the heavenly body that admits of no rival.

> Startled at the solemn warning,
> Let the earth-bound soul arise;
> Christ, her sun, all sloth dispelling,
> Shines upon the morning skies.

There He stands, the single living figure in these three windows, and the highest in the whole church – still recognizably the Galilean, but transfigured, already royal in his red robe, over which hangs a richly embroidered cloak, held in place by a circular jewelled clasp.

I must mention, though reluctantly, Christ's face. It glows with the milk and water of human kindness. And can those hands, so boneless, have wielded a scourge of small cords?

The composition, contrariwise, we cannot but admire, especially the way in which Mr Lane has employed colour to bind the three windows into what is tantamount to a triptych: the vestments of all three figures include the white of purity and the gold of royal association, while red, symbolizing the blood of the 'one, full, perfect and sufficient sacrifice', is worn only by Christ. True, it is also the colour of the angels' wings, but these barely register as such: they serve more as a dark background in contrast to Christ's luminous one. I shall be honest: I at first saw no wings at all, taking them for acanthus leaves, like the ones behind SS John the Evangelist and James in the V & A's Winchester College window, or, nearer to hand, behind Dorcas, to whom we shall shortly be turning.

Our two angels, as sculptures, barely suggest stone. Wax, rather. These windows were best viewed from outside, where, all detail lost, less is more.

The Charity Window

(The west lancet on the south side of the chancel)

The choir stalls, not yet envisaged when this glass was made, hamper a close look. But that hardly matters because the figures – Charity, a baby she is carrying and a little boy – are conceived in terms of mass. But there will be no reading the inscription without binoculars. Let me hand you mine:

TO THE GLORY OF GOD AND IN MEMORY OF
JULIA BAZELY WHO FELL ASLEEP AT AMBERLEY
Feb 3rd 1917 THIS WINDOW IS PLACED HERE
BY HER NEPHEWS AND NIECES ✠ ✠

In the parish magazine for May, 1909, we read:

' . . . Mr. H[enry]. Harwood was re-elected People's Warden, and Mrs. Bazely was nominated by the Vicar as his Warden. Mrs. Bazely is the first lady who has held the office of Churchwarden, and none will dispute that the honour paid her is well deserved. For a quarter of a century she has been the Lady Bountiful of the Parish, and has earned the love and honour of all classes.'

A model of charity herself, she left money so that every child attending Amberley Church School should be given a bun and an orange on breaking up for Christmas, if such could be conveniently obtained, or, if not, some other suitable form of food, the total cost of which should not exceed thirty shillings. Her husband John, Rector of North Stoke, had died in 1880, whereupon she came to live at Westfield House, now Rhiw. Her elevation to the rank of Vicar's Warden did not deter the Bishop of Chichester from continuing to preface his circular letter to the churchwardens of the diocese, 'Gentlemen'.

In treating the Clarkson Windows I mentioned how Mr Lane had resolved the problem of a single figure in a tall, narrow lancet. In the Charity Window the canopy and base are again large, but somewhat more consonant with the simple lancet. Moreover, a single standing figure has been rejected in favour of two, and these overlap vertically, if only to a small degree. This speaks of painting rather than sculpture. In the Cana Window we shall find that the overlap is multiple and many times greater, while the canopy has been pierced almost out of existence. We shall find that the Dorcas Window is compositionally closer to the Charity Window.

Unfortunately the nethermost line of the inscription in the Charity Window is obscured by an 8 cm ledge at the top of the nether slope of the splay. The window being so long and narrow, this is the most inexcusable of errors. Was the designer so transfixed by his own cartoon that he lost all thought of where the glass would go? His pictorial eye-level is certainly high – it runs through Charity's head – whereas the actual eye-level is below the window. Well? He was just adopting a conventional strategy whereby he might lead our attention to some chief feature. In fact the perspective is dual, for the base of the fictive niche sports a scroll – swaggering, *bombé* – which is clearly seen from beneath. The fault lies elsewhere, with that little ledge: it has been built up with a layer of cement – the purpose, quite clearly, being to hold the frame of the glass in its rebate. Understood. But there was no need for it to be given a horizontal surface. If only it slanted downwards, all would be well.

On the aforementioned scroll is written this text from 1 Cor. xiii,13:

The Greatest of these is
CHARITY

And in the right-hand bottom corner of the window:

W. MORRIS & CO
105 ROCHESTER ROW
WESTMINSTER

Near the top are two horizontal ovals. In one of them is written 'IHS' and in the other 'XPC'. These are Greek: iota eta sigma and chi rho sigma, an abbreviation of *Iesous Christos*. Above them is a crown. This is saying that Christ is king, or that charity is the crowning virtue. Or both.

The finely robed Charity cradles a baby in her left arm. Her right hand, no less tenderly, reaches down to the uplifted right hand of a boy who, though facing us, looks up at her. Under her guidance he is walking through his formative years. His uniform is that of a charitable institution, not necessarily the Green Coat School; but green is the colour of his tunic.

*   *   *

Need I say that this window is not by the Pre-Raphaelite polymath but by another William Morris? Though the fictive niche is in a late-gothic style, the three figures that occupy it are *post*-Raphaelite, deeply indebted to the Umbrian master. And not only as to style: Raphaelesque is the composition in the shape of an inverted S, which runs from Charity's head *via* the baby to the dexter side of the charity boy as far as his right foot. Moreover, both Charity and the boy overlap the sides of the fictive niche, something that would never have happened in mediaeval glass.

In the fifteenth and sixteenth centuries a great many Graeco-Roman statues were unearthed, influencing not only sculptors but also painters. These stained glass figures are not without a sculptural quality. On the other hand they are polychrome, which Renaissance statuary typically was not. But Renaissance painting was.

And what is the setting for these figures which smack of Raphael and his school? A late gothic niche! Does that make you laugh? I doubt it, admirer as you are of the niches around Or San Michele.

The Cana Window

(The middle lancet on the south side of the chancel)

As this window has no choir stalls in front of it, it can be see from near, which is fortunate because the scene is a wedding reception, and, as we would expect, contains more figures than any other in the entire church: seven, the perfect number. Inevitably they are mostly small. There are also seven jars, and from one of them a boy is pouring water into another.

Two vines, as at West Hoathly, refer to Christ's words, 'I am the true vine,' and represent the sacrifice of blood, which is here adumbrated by Christ's changing water into wine. As a framing device they operate similarly to the crowns in the Clarkson Windows, climbing up the sides and meeting at the top. There are mediaeval precedents for this, but not for the inclusion of roots. Roots we associate with the fantastic Rackham, but these derive from the Arts and Crafts Movement at its most restrained.

Behind Christ, who wears a wine-red robe, is His mother, and behind *her*, seated at table, the bride and bridegroom, who are the culminating point in the serpentine composition. On either side of them is a man, representing the assembled guests, just as the angels in the Clarkson Window represent the heavenly host. Through their heads runs the pictorial eye-level, far above our own, quite as high as in the Charity Window; but the perspective is again dual: a second pictorial eye-level runs just below the band that curls across the base of the niche. It says:

TO THE HONOUR AND GLORY OF GOD AND IN LOVING MEMORY OF ✧ THE REV D RICHARD MACDONALD CAUNTER AND ANN HIS WIFE ✧ WHO WERE MARRIED IN THIS CHURCH MARCH 21ST 1840

Mr Caunter came from Amberley. A scholar of Sidney Sussex College, Cambridge, he was rector successively of Hanwell and Drayton, both in Oxfordshire. His *Attila, a tragedy, and other poems*, was published in 1832.

*   *   *

As in the Charity Window, and in consequence of the same thoughtlessness, the nethermost line of this inscription is obscured.

Running across the top and middle of the base in two quite widely separated lines is a single text from *Psalms* xvi, 12:

IN THY PRESENCE IS THE FULNESS OF JOY AND AT THY RIGHT HAND THERE IS PLEASURE FOR EVERMORE

Amberley Church

Given the compositional and perspectival similarities between this window and the Charity one, we can only regard their juxtaposition as felicitous. Both, moreover, are about love. But there are also differences: the figures in the Charity Window, as is typical of *our* Morris, possess the rich colours and full plasticity of Italian sixteenth-century painting, whereas those in the Cana Window have the character we associate with stained glass of the late-gothic period, that of a coloured drawing.

Equally late-gothic in style are the backgrounds in both windows. Nonetheless, each has its own character: the fictive niche of the Charity Window, though shallow, is as solidly rounded as the figures it contains. That of the Cana Window looks relatively flat, which is paradoxical, its recession being much greater, thanks largely to the diminishing scale of the figures as they reach ever further back through a palace without walls. At the same time they adhere to the convention of mediaeval painting, whereby scale depends on importance. Observe how this operates: the smallest and furthest are the anonymous bridal couple and two equally anonymous guests; larger and nearer is the mother of Jesus, and, larger and nearer still, Jesus Himself. The illusion of perspective has failed to distort the hierarchical reality.

Dash me! I have overlooked the nearest of all, the water-pouring servant. In order that his scale may be commensurate with his lowly status he has to be a mere boy.

Despite such recession, the designer's starting point is the formal device of a fictive niche. Oh, I grant you that it has no back, but we can confidently say, 'Here is a canopy, here are the sides, here is the base,' metamorphosed though they may be into an architectural fantasy – which we accept: an architectural fantasy is what the late-gothic niche has ever tended to be.

Decorative Elements

The Dorcas Window

(The east lancet of the south aisle)

This window being lower, nothing can obstruct the inscription:

In loving memory of Nina Sanger Easter 1915

Though Mrs Sanger, of St Leonards, never lived in Amberley, she knew the wife of the vicar, the Reverend George Frederick Carr, was generous to the parish and is buried in the churchyard. The window was a gift from her husband. In the right-hand bottom corner is the monogram of the designers, Clayton & Bell. It incorporates the date, 1915.

Here again, and for the last time, we meet a fictive late-gothic niche. This one serves as a frame for Dorcas, who appears in *The Acts of the Apostles*, chapter ix, verses 36–42, though rarely in stained glass. (Sussex has a second one in Berwick.) She was 'full of good works and almsdeeds' and made 'coats and garments'. The message of the window is that of Charity all over again. Dorcas, however, is seated and nimbed, and a child faces her, this time a girl. The little fingers of her left hand feel into the cupped palm of the right hand of Dorcas, who, with her left, adjusts the girl's coat. This is of fine materials and elaborate workmanship. No wonder the girl looks up adoringly at her benefactress. The thought may cross one's mind, however, that if this worthy woman had spent less time on embellishment she could have clothed more of the naked. But there is this to bear in mind: as in the Charity Window, the style, despite the neo-gothic halo, is that of the Italian Renaissance, when art tended to convey aristocratic power – and taste. The only real difference is that here we see less of Raphael and discern a tendency that would ultimately lead to the Baroque: note in particular how the decoration inside the canopy is asymmetrical, rising towards the right. This creates a counter-thrust to balance the girl's slight leftward turn. It is towards the left, too, that the lines of her clothing and that of Dorcas tend to rise.

How remarkable that such sophistication should cohabit with a floor that is depicted in plan – sheer primitivism! Or does it say a still life by Cézanne?

The Stott Window

(The stilted, round-headed window in the former north doorway of the nave)

The stained glass, which replaced a plain window, has buckled, so the composition appears to be fractionally more crowded than was intended. But of course it was somewhat crowded even when flat; on purpose, no doubt: homage is hereby paid to that defining characteristic of mediaeval art, the *horror vacui*.

Below the crown of the arch a scroll bears this legend:

To the GLORY of GOD
and in memory of
EDWARD STOTT ARA
Born April 25 1855 Died in
this Parish March 19 1918

In the right-hand bottom corner is written:

This window
was erected
as a Token
of Affection
by his friend
Anne Dinnage
and was designed
& carried out by

Decorative Elements

his friend Robert
Anning Bell
1919

Of the church's decorative features none is half so celebrated as this. It is the only stained glass in the north wall, and, at that memorable instant of opening the south door, we see no other – anywhere. Eventually, of course, we do. But what is always known as 'the Stott Window' retains a certain uniqueness. For one thing, it is the only stained glass in our church (perhaps in any) which is wider than it is high. It thus allows for the most important figure in the design to be a semi-horizontal one, while those in all the other windows, even if seated, are vertical.

More importantly, however, it differs in *stimmung*: it is both tragic and comic, while the other windows are neither.

Artists without number have lived and worked in Amberley. Nevertheless, if we say 'the Amberley artist' we can only mean Stott. The wide and ignorant world may speak of a second Stott, whose Christian name, if I remember rightly, was William; but he knew not Amberley, and Amberley knows not him. For us there is only one Stott: Edward.

Edward Stott, ARA, the son of a Lancashire mill owner, made Amberley his home. He lived in Stott's Cottage, which is now known as Stott's Corner, presumably on the analogy of Shaw's Corner, the sage of Ayot St Lawrence's Hertfordshire home.

Stott bought other houses in the village, and these he let, though not to make money – the bank would doubtless have recompensed him better: his aim was to thwart the modernizer.

Anne Dinnage, to whom we owe not only this window but also the Stott Monument in the churchyard, was his housekeeper. There is a marble bust of her by Francis Derwent Wood, RA. She inherited

Stott's Corner and eventually sold it to the widow of Sir William Reid Dick, RA (1878–1961).

Stott's paintings of the village and its surroundings were idyllic rather than literal, but in his day the community was still a farming one, hence itself something of an idyll – until the modern world began encroaching, try though he might to prevent it. He painted *time* that was unbounded and *space* that was localized, so one can see why he and telegraph wires were sworn foes. The wires won. Increasingly, therefore, he took refuge in biblical subjects. One of these, the Titianesque *Entombment* of 1915, is the source of the central subject in the round-headed window that celebrates him. Even here, however, Amberley is a flint's throw away.

Inside St Michael's we have already seen the sky of Amberley through clear glass, and Heaven in the central Clarkson window. The Stott Window includes a patch of lattice-work, which is an opaque rendering of an English sky, and a very pale one, too. In actual fact the quarries are of various colours, suggesting that Anning Bell had been studying Monet's divided touch, but unless you scrutinize them carefully they register as being all the same – a leaden over-castness within the leadlines. Ironically, this admits more light than the deep blue of a sunlit sky would have done.

The figure on the left side of the window is an unidealized farm labourer, short, bald, getting on in years. The dead Christ, whom he is helping to carry, is another local man, elevated to the heroic nude. So far so conventional. But there is one thing missing: I am not referring to the halo, which we would hardly expect to find in a work that leans heavily on the High Renaissance, but to the stigmata. I believe that a dead Christ with no wounds in hands, feet and right side is exclusive to this window. They are present, I hasten to add, in Stott's painting. Why not in the stained-glass version, then?

Anning Bell was at work on this window when the First World War had only just ended, so he might have wanted to generalize Christ, the image of sacrifice, as the fallen. The Parochial Church Council had considered a memorial window, only to reject it. Maybe *The Entombment* fulfils this rôle. Indeed Stott himself, painting in 1915, may already have been paying tribute to those who had died at the front. His inclusion of the stigmata does not quash this possibility: they could symbolize myriad mortal wounds. That would explain the man standing at the rear in both the painting and the stained glass.

And an explanation is indeed demanded. The women, by contrast, are the ones we would expect to find here – the Blessed Virgin Mary and the Magdalen. But among the men there is no Nicodemus, St John the Evangelist, St Joseph of Arimathea or St Joseph the husband of Mary. Instead, besides two bearers, there is this iconographical oddity, a Roman soldier.

Have you ever seen a Roman soldier in an *Entombment* before? Greybearded, he can only be that centurion, present at the foot of the cross, who said, 'Truly this was the Son of God.' To the two Maries there is a stoical impassivity, but this company commander – he would make a good model for the Eternal Father – is the mourner with whom we identify. Because of his bulk? Partially, no doubt. But what stays with us is his anguish at seeing a piece of clay that only hours previously had been a man. A man that he himself had sent over the top? Try doubting it. Here is the *Pietà* of Fathers 4 Justice.

In the painting, which is landscape-shaped, this veteran of imperial wars holds a spear in his left hand, but it has been omitted from the rounded window because there was no room for its head – also, perhaps, for fear that we might associate it with one of Christ's wounds, and ask why all five have been omitted.

The thought has struck me that this Christ might also be the *homo amberleianus*, who subsisted between Wildbrooks that were too wet for pasture and Downs that were too steep for plough. This would tally with the lifelong tenor of Stott's work. But what if I was right in suggesting that Golgotha had been so generalized that all the warriors who lay dead in the Great War were subsumed into this one corpse? There need be no incompatibility: the war poems that endure are those that treat of feelings known to Civvy Street.

*　　*　　*

Stott borrowed not only from Titian, who brought *impasto* to oil painting, but also from Corot, for whom colour came after tone. If only such *malerisch* techniques had not been replicated by Anning Bell in the very different medium of stained glass! Upon my soul, could he not have learnt from the formalized folds in our other windows?

Even less aptly, across the foreground there stretches a colourless corpse, shaded into anatomical correctness.

The landscape, on the other hand, has been much more freely interpreted: in the original painting there are distant and hazy trees, but in the window they have been reduced to a clear-cut pattern of outsize leaves. Similarly the pale distance has become a blue of such depth as is never seen in Nature, but only, thanks to Perugino, in art.

*　　*　　*

No fictive niche surrounds the central subject but a border of the kind to be found in thirteenth-century windows, which in turn derived from illuminated manuscripts. This device, so remote from late-gothic sophistication, may be called primitive; and in the stretch along the bottom of the window it is somewhat primitive in actual style. But as we follow it around the inside of the arch, we discover that it has borrowed from fifteen-century Florence, which until quite recently was considered late mediaeval. Throughout the border these styles are subsumed into Anning Bell's own, a more modern one than

Stott's, even in depicting Heaven, where the debt to Botticelli is undisguised. Especially modern is the bottom stretch of border – none more so in the entire church, even though there are works of more recent date.

This window is a lesson in the do's and don'ts of stained glass. Where Anning Bell errs, he has been loyal to the style of his recently deceased friend. Both artists successfully combine the religious with the local. Moreover, there is an effective contrast between Stott's leaden sky of England and Anning Bell's cloudless one of Heaven. In the latter, which curls around the inside of the arch, five demi-angels, brown-haired, sing or play. Or both. Childlike, pure, they look good in haloes, which, though no two are the same, all shine. But (heavens!) they have been infiltrated by a tubby, blond shepherd – from Amberley, you may be sure, and, unlike the demi-angels, unquestionably male. Having elbowed his way into Heaven, he has the effrontery to kit himself with a pair of wings, with a halo even, which, incongruously peach-coloured, gives the game away. But he has jettisoned his round-frock – it smells of linseed oil – and donned angelic garb, which is fortunately loose-fitting, though he goes too far in painting crosses on it: they look like the arrow loops in the curtain wall of the castle. He is blowing an instrument, not a whistle-pipe – it is too bulbous for that – more probably a cornet; I mean the ur-cornet, a horn pure and simple, as played by shepherds ever since sheep began; or maybe it is the cornet of court circles, the wooden variety, whose heyday was the sixteenth and seventeenth centuries. In 1638 it was described as 'like a ray of sunshine piercing the shadows, when heard with the choir voices in the cathedrals or chapels.' Well, let us think the best we can of our Amberley shepherd. It is the *bona fide* demi-angels who are a worry: two play the cymbals, one a curved pipe. What a charivari that must be! Better, perhaps, than the 'horn-fair' or 'rough music' to which our church band – 'musicianers', they called themselves – treated a vicar of ours after they had refused to play the hymns, and he had retaliated by refusing to preach. Even so, scarcely what we understand by angelic harmony. Or is such to God's taste? 'Praise him upon the well-tuned cymbals,' says the psalmist. And he should know. We find two cymbal-playing angels on the choir screen of York Minster.

*   *   *

Immediately below this heaven of demi-angels, on either side, is a sibyl. Each is framed by an arch, a Roman one, or at any rate semicircular, like the window itself. And these too finish at the waist.

The left-hand one is labelled 'ART' and carries a scroll on which is written '"The Life so short the Art so long to lerne"', which is the first line of *The Parlement of Foules* – except that 'Lyf' has been amended to 'Life', for spelling was not Chaucer's forte. This is a translation of Hippocrates' aphorism, ὁ βίος βραχύς ἡ δὲ τέχνη μακρή (Over the fireplace in the upstairs drawing-room of Philip Webb's Red House, Bexley Heath (1859), we find 'ARS LONGA VITA BREVIS'.)

The right-hand sibyl is labelled 'NATURE' and carries a scroll on which is written '*Laborare est Orare*', a tag the shepherds might well have adopted as their motto: all too often they would miss church rather than leave their flocks, especially in lambing time. This augured ill for their eternal welfare. On dying, therefore, they were buried with a lock of wool in each hand: the Judge of the earth, thus apprized of their calling, will lean towards mercy. If only Stott, under his monument in the churchyard, had a brush in his right hand, a rectangular palette in his left! It is only right that this sedulous artist's oeuvre should tip the scales in his favour! Nor am I referring exclusively to his religious paintings, for his scenes of Amberley and the Wildbrooks are also in a sense religious: this cul-de-sac village, bypassed by the highroad of modernity, is Paradise on earth –

threatened, to be sure, but not yet lost. In Stott's rendition it is Nature as God intended. And Man? He is at one with her, as he is with the animals, and, doubtless, with St Michael too, indeed with all the company of Heaven.

What am I on about? Is not this fustian? Gas? Gush? Much cry and little wool? You might say that the Amberley farm labourer, out at all hours, in all weathers, knew Hell. But there is no Hell in Stott, only a harsh Heaven. Thus *The Entombment* is an idyllic landscape, an overcast sky and the slaughtered Lamb. *Et in Arcadia Ego.*

Observe how the treatment of the sibyls' drapery contrasts with that in all the other windows: Anning Bell, courteously enough, has approximated it to that in *The Entombment*, but with a saving difference: the folds have been lightly sketched. In consequence they war not with the medium of stained glass. These representations of 'Art' and 'Nature' chime with the angels in the Clarkson Windows: here too the right-hand one ('Nature') looks straight ahead, while the left-hand one ('Art') turns towards Christ; and perhaps one should also say to the painting of Him – to Stott in other words, of whom she approves. In him Art and Nature are one. That is why the two sibyls are as like one another as the two angels in the Clarkson Windows.

The bottom stretch of border, consisting of three scenes, is something of a predella. On either side are beasts and poultry that in Stott's day were met in greater numbers than now, even along the lanes and in the yards of the village itself. At the centre is Michael, our tutelary angel, who thrusts his sword into the Dragon. Here – here especially – Anning Bell plays with Stott's combination of the religious and the local. The play is serious, of course, but it includes a little joke: our patron saint has the blond hair of the shepherd who gatecrashed Heaven, but, with careworn eyes, he is a generation older. In the war against Satan and his tribe – the celestial war to end all celestial wars – he was no recruit but the angelic host's general-in-chief, as old as Stott's centurion. The strain shows, we see every Caravaggesque furrow, for we are allocated a ringside seat. The fight is a victorious one, oh yes indeed. But victory, observed from close to, is scarcely distinguishable from defeat; 'for every battle of the warrior is with confused noise, and garments rolled in blood.'

Michael we expect to see as a young hero, suave and implacable, like that Calvary-bound Christ in the mural, who, you will recall, took everything in His stride: He it is who had something of the young warrior-angel about Him. And this prince of the heavenly host? An aging man of sorrows, acquainted with grief.

The earthly paradise of animals on either side, the celestial one of angels above, create both setting for, and commentary on, the strife. Despite all the differences, Stott's *Entombment* and Anning Bell's border are fundamentally saying the same thing.

*   *   *

E. Liddall Armitage wrote in *Stained Glass*, 1959:

> Robert Anning Bell, RA, RWS, RBC, LLB, added distinction to the stained glass craft with his excellent sense of design and fine draughtsmanship. For a time he was professor of design at the Royal College of Art and also in the Glasgow School of Art.
>
> A delightful window of his may be seen in the Parish Church of Amberley, Sussex, designed in memory of Edward Stott, RA [sic] . . .

Stott missed becoming an RA by one vote.

The St Edith Window

(A pair of lancets in the south aisle to the east of the porch)

Leaving the Stott Window we are once again in the world of upright figures and the lancet – of two in fact, for this window is a diptych. Here we revert to the single figures we found in the Clarkson

Windows, except that in the right-hand light there is a slice of a second one, who is cut by the frame. Both are angels. Between them there protrudes a pair of wings that can only belong to a third. If you doubt me, cast your eyes down and you will discover that there are three right feet.

The surplus space over their heads is largely devoted to landscape, which, like the overlapping of figures in the Charity, Cana and Dorcas Windows, is a pictorial solution, whereas the niche is architectural-sculptural.

Near the bottom of both lights is a scroll. On the left one:

In memory of Edith Octavia
Jennings of Amberley House
Died in Florence June 4th 1931.

And on the right:

Be of good courage and He
Shall strengthen your heart
All ye that hope in the Lord
[*Psalm* xxxi, 24]

Edith Jennings was an unmarried American who lived partially at Il Poderino, her family's Florentine villa, and partially at Amberley House with her niece Gladys Huntington, whose husband Constant, also American, was in charge of the London office of Putman's.

*   *   *

Sequestered as I am in this Downland village, I may be parochial in my judgment, but I can only say that this window strikes me as one of the most beautiful anywhere. A gift of Edith Jennings's sister, Mrs Alfred Parrish, it is by Veronica Whall (1887–1967) and was inserted in 1933 – despite the opposition of an Amberley artist, Elsa Noele

Dalglish, of Easter Bartons, now Easter Barton, who found it too modern. I have no doubt on the other hand that you, sophisticated reader, will maintain that it is not modern enough; and there can be no denying that it is more than a little neo-gothic. But the lady had a point: turn your eyes ninety degrees leftwards to revisit the Dorcas Window, then back again: Whall's colours are different from Clayton & Bell's: they are applied with the smoothness of a Walter Crane; they would sit well on a motorcyclist's helmet.

How come, then, that her panes should be so archaically small? Her predecessors only used leadlines because they had to. She, however, makes a virtue of necessity: in her hands they outline the forms with rudimentary emphasis and at the same time resolve them into semi-abstraction. Concentrate on them, dear reader, isolating them from the glass. You will find your effort repaid, I think. If, however, your eye fails to cooperate, step into the churchyard and look at them from there.

*   *   *

In essence this pair of windows is Art Deco, and only neo-gothic in so far as the figures simulate polychrome statues in fictive niches – niches, however, that are no more than vestigial, having almost been schematized out of existence: they have neither back nor sides; the bases have been simplified into plain quarry glass, and the scrolls that flutter across them, though faithful to tradition, could only be modern. The canopies, as one would expect, are more complex: here again is quarry glass, but it has been played around with. It jitterbugs. And it is rendered all the jerkier by several lozenges of bright colour, which are purely abstract, quite unrelated to the sky in which they are set, though integral to the design. This sky, I imagine, was inspired by the one in the Stott Window, for here again we have panes of different colours, all pale, combining to create a leaden cloudiness. But whereas

Decorative Elements

Anning Bell was interpreting the sky in *The Entombment,* Whall chose hers freely: conscious of inevitably darkening the interior, she was keen not to do so any more than necessary.

The Christ in the Stott Window was a portrait of a local man; here, in the left-hand light of what is tantamount to a single window, St Edith or Eadgyth (961?-984), a nun of Wilton, is a portrait of Edith Jennings. But there the similarity ends: this patrician lady was only local up to a point, and no child of the soil. Moreover, she was painted not from life but from a photograph, and an old one at that, dating from her early twenties – the age at which St Edith died. But even when elderly she maintained her upright bearing: a lancet would never have experienced difficulty in accommodating her. With her perfect mouth, strong jaw and somewhat sunken eyes she was a formidable figure.

St Edith, having promised a couple that she would act as god-mother to their child, died before it was born; but she did not allow such a detail to stand in her way. Occupying the left light, she wears a crown, despite being born to King Edgar out of wedlock. Even more incongruously, she carries a crozier: she declined to become abbess of her nunnery, preferring, we are told, 'to serve her sisters in the most humble capacities, like Martha herself'. We must remember, however, that we see her in Heaven, where the last shall be first. As a saint she is abbess and more, her crown a spiritual one.

The thought occurs to me that I might not unhesitatingly entrust my baby to the arm of a ghost; but then, on turning to the right-hand light, I discover how wrong I would be, for behold, angels in bright raiment attend her. It is good to have angels at a baptism: there are four round the font at St Mary's, Ware. Here one and a bit, and the vestige of a third; there are only three, but, like the two in the Clarkson Windows, they represent the heavenly host, and they are similarly dressed, for these equally perform a quasi-sacerdotal rôle, being in attendance on an ecclesiastical superior. Their feet, however, are bare: it is royal St Edith who has golden shoes.

The sky is English. The background, on the other hand, is Italian, dominated by the olives and cypresses that Edith Jennings could see from her Tuscan villa. In the right-hand light we catch a glimpse of an ancient building, which presumably represents the nunnery at Wilton.

The High Altar

The font is placed against a pier. The high altar, as if one error could cancel out another, is freestanding. Its Anglo-Norman predecessor marked the midpoint along the cord of the apse, saying, 'Anywhere but here were exile.' And the Early English one, standing against the flat end of our Early English chancel, saw the roll moulding nod in agreement as it uttered the very same words. But although its dislodgement detracts from the church's axial perspective, it is less than ruinous. Even so, one says, 'Why here, precisely?' Not by a hair's breadth should the siting of an altar seem arbitrary.

*   *   *

There was a reason for its being roughly there, though: the priest wanted to celebrate with his face to the congregation, or, as he said if in need of ancient credentials, *more romano*. But there is no precedent for facing west: the early Christian basilicas had the altar at the west end, so the priest, in facing the congregation, faced east. In churches with their altars at the east end he faced the same way as the congregation, in oneness with them, and so he or she still does at our side altar.

Altars, from early times, have been either tomblike or tablelike, whether of stone or of wood. Our own high altar, designed by J.R. Penman in 1968 and installed the following year, is tablelike and of stone, though in the slenderness of the design it nods at wood. Across either end it even has a floor-hugging stretcher, whose upper surface, on the other hand, curves gently upwards towards the calves of the legs, and there is nothing un-stone-like about *that*; nor, one may add, about an answering (but steeper) curve that descends arcuately from the mensa. Observe that there is neither base nor capital to mark these junctions. Simplicity itself! – comparable with the arcade around the font; or, in the mural, the arches below the tomb from which Christ rises. (This had been brought to light only a year previously.) Capitals are to be found elsewhere, at the top of the legs: they derive from the cushion type, a sphere that interpenetrates a cube, creating a lunette on each of its four sides, but pared down, in keeping with the altar's general lines.

Not unlike John Skelton's font in Chichester Cathedral, this altar operates as a sculpture, abstract and modern – with a nod at Romanesque. Less happy, however, is the arcaded decoration round the mensa, which borrows from the heads of lancets, with circles for hanging capitals. In contrast to the breadth of design that governs the altar as a whole, this stands out as frilly: a stone quarry meets Bond Street. Is it telling us that the stone was prepared in Portland, the frieze carved in London? We could do with an altar cloth that hangs down over the mensa: frills were best left to lace.

It was on the installation of this new altar that our vicar, under the influence of the Second Vatican Council, began to face west, thereby turning his back on many centuries of Catholic practice.

Flooring

A small amount of the pre-1864 flooring survives, but it has been displaced: our one monumental brass is on the wall of the south aisle, and a few stone slabs, originally in the body of the church, now pave the porch. Following the great reparation, Minton tiles, red, black and buff, were laid in the chancel, and, except where there were benches, in the nave and south aisle. The designs are either abstract or abstractly floriate. Clarkson writes: 'A pavement . . . has been laid by Mr. England, of Bury Place, Bloomsbury, mosaic artist, the Rev. the Lord Alwyne Compton having furnished some effective designs.'

In the chancel – unfortunately, but inevitably – the outer border of lozenges has been encroached upon by the subsequent panelling. At present this only affects the choir, or that fraction of it where there are no stalls, for in the sanctuary, ever since 1960, a carpet has been laid, wall to wall. From the Persian rug, which, in the late Middle Ages, served as a celebrant's mat on the better class of altar pace, we have declined to a sell-by-the-metre floor-covering. However, it will eventually reach the end of its unnatural life, whereupon the tiles, which are of the same pattern as those in the nave, will, with luck, be re-exposed.

Tablets

Like St Michael's itself, the tablets tend to be simple, as are the inscriptions, for the local poetaster has taken Keats to heart:

> O 'tis a very sin
> For one so weak to venture his poor verse
> In such a place as this.

All is prose, and English prose at that, even when in tribute to lettered divines. The exception is the mediaeval Sir John Wantele, who merits two lines of abbreviated Latin, and on whose soul may God have mercy. In recent ages he might have been joined by scores of other worthies, but there are happily no more than eight.

Half of these have unproudly chosen to remain outside and confront the Russian wind. And they are carved in the most fugitive of stone. All are eighteenth century, all on the end wall of the chancel. They commemorate the Reverend Bell Carleton – during whose incumbency, appropriately enough, our bells were cast and hung – and members of his family. The inscriptions, from left to right, are as follows:

Here
Lyeth intered the Body of
MARY CARLETON
who Died January the 25
1740
Aged 18 Years, & 4 Months
[Here] also Lyeth ye Body of
Sarah wife of Bell Carleton

Vicar of this Parish who
died May the 20th 1746
Aged 56
Here also Lyeth ye Body of
Bell Carleton AM Rector
of Angmering and Vicar
of this Parish who died
June the 23d 1746
Aged 54
*

Sacred
to the memory of
CATHERINE Wife of
RICHD BETTESWORTH Esqr
of Woollavington Sussex and
Youngest Daughter of the
Revd BELL CARLETON AM
formerly Vicar of this Parish
She died [universa]lly respected
and esteemed July 25th 1795
In the 73d Year of her age
as a tribute of affection
this monument was erected
by her Niece
MARY GROOM
*

'Here Lyeth interred
the Body of
JOHN HAMMOND
who died the 25th
of August 1747
Aged 56 Years
*

Tablets

To
the Memory of
RHODA the Widow of
Mr JOHN HAMMOND
and Eldest Daughter
of the late
Rev BELL CARLETON
[who died]
[the] 7 of December 1790
Aged 75 Years.

*   *   *

One of the two tablets that were removed upon the erection of the clasping buttresses survives, having been re-erected inside the nave, on the west wall, near the right-hand corner. It reads:

Here lieth Interr'd
the Body of
EDWARD ELLIOTT
Who died
the 7th of April 1782
Aged 55 Years.

To the left of it, on the other side of the tower door, is a stone by Eric Gill, ARA (1882–1940), that bears this legend:

JOAN MARY
STRATTON
DIED APRIL 1919
AGED 17 YEARS
✠

DEAR CHILD.

She was the younger daughter of Fred Stratton (1870–1960), an artist who lived at Boxtree Cottage, now Boxwood. His son Hilary, who studied under Gill, became a fellow of the Royal Society of British Sculptors.

The Diocesan Registrar expressed his disapproval of the words 'Dear child'. The vicar, the Reverend Herbert Rickard, retorted, ' . . . Mr Stratton pointed out to me that it is merely using in the singular an expression which S. Paul uses in the plural.' ('Be ye therefore followers of God, as dear children.' *Ephesians* v, 1) A pious thought. But there is nothing about 'Dear child' to which the devoutest unbelievers could object. On the other hand her profile, a roundel in low relief, evokes Gill's Madonnas. And it echoes our other isolated head, the round fragment of mural from *The Visitation* in the south aisle, uncovered forty-seven years later.

As in Gill's engravings, the hair is conveyed by parallel lines. Indeed the whole roundel is not unlike an engraving, the relief being so low – as low as in the blind arcade around the font.

You are touched by this portrait, are you not? Would you be touched if you had not read the inscription? I like to think so.

*   *   *

To the left of the south door, as if in expectation that a second one would eventually balance it on the right, is a bronze plate, by G. Maile & Son, in which are incised the names of those who fell in the First World War, 1914–18. When another had to be made for the fallen of the Second World War, 1939–45, the Diocesan Advisory Committee accepted that it should be of the same design, much as they disliked it. I see nothing wrong with it.

*   *   *

To the right of the St Edith Window is a copper plaque, etched with the names of the known vicars of Amberley and the dates of their incumbency, from 1370 to 1993. It is by Gerald Burns (1862–1945), who lived at The Studio, now 'The Old Studio'. This is not to be confused with the little house by the gates to Carlisle House, which is *now* called 'The Studio', where he also worked. Known principally as an etcher, he specialized in architectural and marine subjects. At the bottom of the plate he left room for further names, and this is now full. Suffixed on a framed sheet of paper is a list of 'priests in charge', as incumbents are now called. It is a polite way of saying that they have been denied the freehold.

*   *   *

In the chancel there are only two tablets. They are symmetrically situated on the side walls above the sanctuary rail. There is also a symmetry to the persons commemorated, Hanley and Clarkson, the longest-serving vicars of Amberley and transfluvial Houghton. Between them they reigned over us for a little more than a century. But not quite consecutively: they were divided by the shortest-serving, the Reverend John Charles Favell Tufnell: he resigned after three weeks.

First on the north side:

TO
THE REVD JOHN HANLEY
FORTY FIVE YEARS VICAR OF
AMBERLEY CUM HOUGHTON
IN THE COUNTY OF SUSSEX
WHO DIED 26TH FEBRUARY 1840
AGED 82 YEARS
THIS TABLET IS DEDICATED
IN SACRED AND GRATEFUL REMEMBRANCE

Amberley Church

BY DONALD AND ANN CAUNTER.
ENTER NOT INTO JUDGMENT WITH THY
SERVANT O LORD.
PS. CXLIII. 2.

This tablet, the most elegant object in Amberley, bestrides the Regency and the young Victoria. White marble is set on black slate with a rectangular base, rounded shoulders and a pedimental head. Two triple mouldings surround the inscription. At the apex is a three-armed Moline cross, standing on a square base. On either side, in the upper half, is an empty, gable-roofed niche on a moulded base, supported by a triangular ornamental bracket. The lettering is at one with the tablet itself, being black-filled Roman, except for the first word, which, like the niches, is gothic. These two contrasting styles are not unrelated to those of the church itself, Anglo-Norman and Early English. The designer was Thomas Rice, whom Rupert Gunnis includes in *Dictionary of British Sculptors*. Incised in the right-hand bottom corner of the slab is 'RICE: BROMPTON MIDX.'

This tablet is reflected, though far from replicated, by the one on the opposite wall:

IN LOVING MEMORY OF
THE REVD GEORGE ARTHUR CLARKSON M.A.
FOR FIFTY-SEVEN YEARS VICAR
OF AMBERLEY-CUM-HOUGHTON 1840–1897,
DIED JULY 18TH 1897
AGED 82 YEARS.
'BLESSED ARE THE DEAD WHO DIE IN THE LORD'.
[*Revelation* xiv, 13]

It was placed there in April, 1898, by his widow. Again it is white marble on black slate. Its four corners are all concave, but it chiefly differs from Hanley's in that it is horizontal and in that it is completely plain. It is the only tablet in the entire church that is broader than it is tall.

Sanctuary Rail, Choir Stalls, Organ and Pulpit

In 1215, the year of Magna Carta, the Fourth Lateran Council laid down that the laity were to be denied the chalice. Sacerdotalism, sensitive to the *periculum effusionis*, was reaching its apogee. The chancel, which only fifteen years later was to be so greatly extended, still reflects this, as once did its richness:

> From many a garnished niche around
> Stern saints and tortured martyrs frowned.

Well, not *many*, perhaps. But the Constitutions of Archbishop Winchelsea of Canterbury (1292–1313) require that every chancel should have a frontal for the high altar, a pyx, a Paschal candlestick, a processional cross, a censer, an image of the tutelary saint, and books and vestments for the priest. Enough that the nave should have a font – no pulpit – and the tower a ring of bells.

In or around the year 1500 a foreign visitor wrote about the English that 'above all are their riches displayed in church treasures; for there is not a parish in the kingdom so mean as not to possess crucifixes, candlesticks, censers, patens and cups of silver.'

At Amberley we have never seen the like again, and in the Georgian era our sanctuary even became denuded and abandoned, after which, however, there was some turning of the tide.

*   *   *

The years 1905–09 saw an accretion of dignity through dark oak fittings, all designed by W. D. Caroë, ARIBA.

In 2004 one-cell Wiggonholt Church acquired a new harmonium. So in 1864 had bigger St Michael's, but there was a difficulty. Not that the treadles demand strong legs: Miss Greenfield, the daughter of what was in effect Amberley's Harrods, with its straw skeps and bales of drugget, managed to play ours from 1896 to 1906; but it could hardly make itself heard. On Easter Day, 1903, the choir of eighteen and congregation were accompanied at Matins and Evensong by the Amberley and Houghton Brass Band, and again on the Feast of St Michael and All Angels, which doubled as Harvest Festival. The following year an organ was bought from the Positive Organ Company, and the year after that it received its case, presented by Seymour Ruff, who fitted brass curtain rods. At 2.30 p.m. on Wednesday, 31st May, 1905, began the service of dedication of the new organ, new choir stalls, new sanctuary rail. Despite that, there was ciphering, a problem that the harmonium had never given. In 1962 an electric blower was fitted, since when we have seen no more human blowers, the last of whom was Susanne Slaughter. She had joined the choir at the age of eight. In 1977 the Positive organ was replaced by an electric one, and that by another in 1997.

The sanctuary rail is very unlike those early ones, through whose balusters no dog could squeeze: it simply has eight posts. No, *not* so simply: they are in four pairs, between each of which, under the moulded rail, are finely carved variations on the theme of the quatre-foil. But the congregation is too far away to read such subtleties, except when kneeling to receive communion, which is hardly the moment.

The choir stalls, in two banks on either side, are no less rich, but the style is Jacobean rather than late Gothic. At the west extremity on either side there is a clergy stall with two openings in the front. The choir stalls proper are less elevated. They too have openings, small by comparison, in sets of three: twelve on the south side, but only nine on the north: it is shorter – to allow for the organ. The crowning features were once twelve poppyheads, all different in their carving. But in 1972 someone saw fit to saw them off. Three have vanished. The other nine were sliced through the middle so that the eighteen resulting halves might be fixed to the fronts. Here, believe me, they are intrusive, inappropriate and otiose, bereft of all significance, wrong. The stumps that the amputations had left were smoothed into segmental curves, bland, alien, the epitome of bathos.

This spoliation, for which a faculty was requested and duly granted, is recorded in the parish magazine under the heading 'CHURCH IMPROVEMENTS'. But one day our surviving half-poppyheads, having become whole again, will resume their entitlement, joined by three newly carved ones.

Incidentally, if you see the choir sitting to pray, be merciful: our stalls were not meant for kneeling, unless a sadist designed them.

*   *   *

The organ case, the choir stalls and the sanctuary rail now being of oak (not to mention the lectern) the stained-deal pulpit began to look less dignified than ever. The one we have now, designed in 1908, is a great improvement, except that its stairs rise flush with the base of the chancel arch. Previously they were on the wall side. Like countless pulpits, it is octagonal, on a stone stem, which is octagonal too, thereby confirming beyond doubt that the words of the preacher are an intermediary between the Earth (square) and Heaven (round). It is similar to the sanctuary rail in so far as each motif tends to be regarded as an occasion for inventiveness rather than repetition verbatim. The style, however, differs in that it is not only Gothic but also High Renaissance, if not proto-Baroque, a *mélange* that says 'Elizabethan', much favoured in the Victorian-Edwardian period. Unusual are openings in the sides, which Caroë – an inspired act of self-plagiarism, this – derived from those in the fronts of his choir stalls. Little boys, as soon as the service is over, climb up and stick their heads through them. Little girls never. Five oaken figures, all standing, have been affixed to the solid panels beneath, a gift from Baroness (Evelyn) Emmet of Amberley, JP, who lived in the castle. They are in a Northern Renaissance style and look nineteenth-century. From left to right they are an ecclesiastic with a money-bag, an ecclesiastic at prayer, St John the Baptist (larger than the others), another ecclesiastic at prayer and a shepherd. As St Michael's is low on statuary – not even a St Michael – they constitute welcome additions. There is a brass plaque which you would have overlooked if I had not drawn your attention to it: it is tucked away on the east-facing side. The inscription reads: 'To the glory of God and in loving memory of Henry and Elizabeth Harwood of Amberley Castle. This pulpit was erected by their children, 1909.'

Nearby on the wall there is a wrought-iron hourglass bracket, dating from the eighteenth century, if not earlier. The original hourglass is missing. In September, 1913, a replacement was installed, but this is now missing, too.

*   *   *

The good people of Amberley having been excessive in their contribution to the pulpit fund, the surplus was spent on panelling the three sides of the sanctuary. This stretches from the floor to the roll moulding, with gaps for the aumbrey and the piscina. Stylistically there was no looking back to its Early English setting, only to late Gothic, as with the stained glass in the east windows, which was installed at the beginning of the same decade. (An apter comparison, however, may be with Caroë's own sanctuary rail.) A sequence of slightly sunken panels, basically plain, is trimmed with scroll tracery. Caroë derived this motif from masonry, or rather from fourteenth-century wood-workers who had themselves done so.

Sanctuary Rail, Choir Stalls, Organ and Pulpit

Unlike our other oaken fittings, the panelling is basically simple, nor does it offer any variety, except that the central panel of the east wall is wider than the rest – of four planks instead of three – as wide, be it observed, as the priest's chair. But as this has only been set in front of it since 1968, Fortune played her part. The explanation for the greater width of panel lies elsewhere: previously the high altar stood flush with the wall, and no background incidents were to detract from the cross that stood on it. The altar is now freestanding, and, in accordance with ancient custom, crossless.

*   *   *

The vigil of St John the Baptist's Day, 1909, saw the dedication of both the pulpit and the panelling. In December of the same year the generosity of Alfred Parrish enabled the latter to be extended to the choir. It differs only in that it has no gothic tracery. What does this tell us? That though the choir is holier than the nave, the sanctuary is holier still. Am I implying that our church has thereby been transformed into a three-cell one? Well, I could point to the panelling: the change in it corresponds with the rise in floor level. Unconvinced, are you? You point to the bolection moulding that offers to underpin the original roll moulding. Wood contrasting with stone, complex curves with a simple semi-cylinder, they march past in tandem, as Olympianly indifferent to any break as the windows themselves.

The Positive organ stood against the north wall of the choir, so naturally no panelling was installed there. The present organ is freestanding, with the organist behind it. Consequently the gap in the panelling now shows, and Ronald Burr, our Director of Music from 1994 to 2000, is bequeathing a sum of money to fill it. Let us hope we shall be kept waiting for a very long time.

*   *   *

The Paschal candlestick, of light oak, was designed and made in 1995 by Neill Hill, who was one of our churchwardens from 1998 to 2005.

Seating and Heating

Two things impair the beauty of Amberley Church: congregational seating and heating apparatuses. Both serve the frivolous cause of comfort.

Who invented comfort? One might as well ask who invented long sermons. But perhaps they are linked, for they date from roughly the same era. Previously you would have had the choice of standing or kneeling. In early times you may even have lain prostrate. Only the old and the infirm sat – on a ledge around the wall. But as the Middle Ages progressed, seating, so destructive of clarity and spaciousness, began to fill most western European naves. Amberley, at the very latest, would have acquired some by the time the pulpit window was made, *i.e.*, long before the year 1687, when the Diocesan Survey said this of us: ' . . . the seates are repayred, saving only some few; to whome they belong to repayre they doe not as yet know.' And in 1724: 'The church healing [rendering] on the north side [of the interior] and the floor of the seats want to be mended very much, and the windows are broken.' By then box-pews had been invented, and we see them in that print of 1820: they were in the body of the nave and in the western half of the chancel, the former facing eastwards, the latter westwards – all, that is to say, towards the pulpit – unless there was seating on both sides of some or all of the boxes, a more companionable arrangement: boxes served families rather than individuals, and one could keep an eye on the children. But St Augustine of Hippo must have felt rebuffed: *Cum ad orationem stamus, ad orientem convertimur*. And what would he have said when the hymn started? The whole congregation, whether in the nave or the chancel, turned to face the musicians' gallery at the west end. Here the bandmaster would face them, conducting with his back to the singers and instrumentalists.

*   *   *

In 1864 the box-pews went. Even if they were not fashioned after the horse-box, their name derives from it, so the fact that they ended up as pigs' troughs in not entirely incongruous. The benches that we know – of pine, with canted corners – replaced them in the body of the nave.

Benches even spread to the south aisle, where people were cut off from the action: the clergy and choir had returned to the chancel. In the Middle Ages there had been a side altar, which, even when not in use, had at least acted as a visual aid and as some kind of focus. But these benches reached as far as the east wall, and only in 1967 were the front three removed so that an altar might be reinstated.

In *Notes on Amberley* Clarkson wrote: 'It has been permitted us to see the church attain a condition of marked improvement – a state more worthy of its high and holy purposes, partially developing the ideal of the House of God, as having all things decent and in order – as open, free, common to rich and poor, partakers of common flesh-hood and common blood-hood.' The Georgian hierarchy had been thrown out – literally, in so far as it was dependant on box-pews. Benches, contrariwise, know no obvious pecking-order: a bench is a bench is a bench. On the other hand every member of the Georgian congregation, high or low, had been able to see the parson because he had conducted the service from the pulpit.

*   *   *

Door-openers of box-pews – or 'square-pews', as Clarkson called them, thereby avoiding the equine association, have gone the way of lamp-lighters and linkmen. Benches are doorless. On the other hand they have ends. Moreover, each set of them was originally prefaced by a front. Thus in some degree the concept of a rectangular block survived. At Amberley we have five sets, and they are now all wanting, except for the one that is bordered by the arcade, the west wall and the gangways to north and east.

Of the northernmost set the two rearmost benches and their wooden flooring were removed to make way for a heating apparatus. This has now itself gone, to be replaced by a radiator. But the shelf at the rear of what is *now* the rearmost bench is still *in situ*, forlorn without prayer-books, hymn-books, or children's elbows. In malign compensation the foremost bench invites you to sit, but no shelf precedes it: the front has been removed. There was a reason for this: to make room for the current pulpit, whose sides, unlike those of the previous one, lean outwards. On the other hand the removal of the front to the set of benches between the east wall of the nave and the north-south gangway defies explanation.

The body of the nave cannot compare with the south aisle for benches lost, or space gained, according to your point of view. I have already, with reference to the font, mentioned the area adjacent to the perpendicularized window. The foremost bench and its front are all that remain: they serve as a repository for prayer books and hymn books. To the east of the gangway there are still three benches. A fourth, minus its seat, looks disconcertingly surreal, but acts as a front to the one behind. Its end has been replaced by a narrower one – from the missing front. The side altar has a portable communion rail with a brass plaque that says:

Seating and Heating

DEDICATED TO THE MEMORY OF SEYMOUR RUFF
WHO PASSED AWAY 24TH FEBRUARY 1947
BY HIS NEPHEW AND NIECES.

*   *   *

The raised wooden flooring, except the bit beneath the two benches that were once in the north-west corner, remains intact, even where it no longer has anything to stand on it. The effect is anomalous but informative: we deduce that there were once considerably more benches and fronts than there are now. Smears on the boards would tell us where the missing ones stood, even if their sawn-off tenons were not still fast in their mortises.

The benches, you will remember my saying, are grouped in five sets, four of which have been depredated. Their visual massing has consequently suffered, but I would not so much want them restored to their original state as removed *in toto*. Architecture is the use of solids to create voids, and these were more clearly read when the floor was bare. Besides (and here lies my chief cavil) one can no longer dance.

Angels, unless a thousand painters lie, prefer singing and dancing to go together, which is why 'song and dance' sounds like one word. Carols are ring-dance songs. And when the Sompting Village Morris Dancers perform *Ding dong! Merrily on high*, I defy you – O.K., carry on drinking – not to respond devotionally. 'Let them praise his name in the dance: let them sing praises unto him with tabret and harp.'

*   *   *

Besides benches, our church suffers from another blemish: heating apparatuses. Again your prioritizing of comfort is to blame. If you feel cold, wear more. Still suffering? Then hold a lighted candle.

In 1899 the church acquired 'proper' heating, by which is meant that a stove pipe could go. According to the parish magazine, John

Grundy, of 30 Duncan Terrace, London N, guaranteed 'to keep us as warm as we like in the coldest or dampest weather, nor need we be at all too warm at any other time, which is perhaps quite as important . . . only an iron grating of ornamental designs on the floor will be visible, and no one need look at that unless they wish to do so.'

All was not well, however: when the wind blew from the north the church filled with smoke and the congregation was mightily kippered. In January, 1908, the decision was reached to carry the brick chimney to the top of the tower, or even higher, to prevent the down draught.

In the winter of 1930 the congregation was again smoked out. The firm that had installed the apparatus thirty-one years previously inspected it and reported that it was 'completely worn out and beyond economic repair. Another firm was engaged to come up with a temporary solution.

In the parish magazine for September, 1935, we read: 'The present apparatus is worn out, emits sulphurous and dirty smoke and at best heats only the nave and leaves the chancel in winter thoroughly arctic.'

In December, 1937, a new oil stove was installed, and a new heating system in February, 1948, with indifferent success.

In March, 1954, the Parochial Church Council considered the report of the heating committee and decided that a complete electrical system was beyond their means. The Hon. Mrs Emmet (as she then was) proposed that three new points should be installed. In September two electric heaters were set high up in the south aisle, and in November work began on a McClary Hot Air System. This involved removing those two benches in the north-west corner of the nave and laying a concrete base. No one was yet happy: but paraffin stoves helped.

In 1960 a hot-air system was considered, but the consultant engineer pointed out that the church stands on solid rock, so any excavation for the insertion of ducts would be costly. Instead a hot-*water* system was installed, heated by an oil-fired burner, and was first in operation on Sunday, November 13th. That is why we have pipes snaking round the church like a toy train set, with a tunnel, toot-toot, through the bottom step of the pulpit. Not even the imposts of the chancel arch have been spared. No less intrusive are the radiators, twelve in the body of the church, and one in the ringing chamber. The latter has been set against the west window of the nave, for all to see.

The Churchyard

'Churchyard' has become synonymous with 'graveyard'. If ours has never been without its dead, until recent centuries it was predominantly a place where people met. That was before the Best-kept Village Competition, though as recently as 1981 the judges said of Amberley that they 'liked the sheep in the Churchyard'. But they proved unpopular (the sheep, I mean): they were not nice. Nor were lumps and bumps, which have largely been levelled. But the rabbit, refusing to take a hint, has gone on with its digs, some of which have proved interestingly archaeological.

We have a tombstone from 1700, now set against the west wall of the south aisle, and some eighteenth-century ones. In distant times the tendency was to mark graves with wood – if at all; but we have no surviving examples. In 1912 the Reverend George Frederick Carr, who was vicar at the time, wrote in the parish magazine: 'May we kindly ask our humbler parishioners not to put artificial wreaths on graves until a faculty for doing so has been obtained . . . A simple oak cross with an inscription is all that is needed to mark a grave. The Vicar feels he has the support of his parishioners in his endeavours to prevent their beautiful old English churchyard from being vulgarized by those cheap and nasty substitutes for tombstones . . . They are practically indestructible.'

Indestructible is what oak, however, could never be called – not at least in our beautiful old English weather – and no such crosses have survived, if indeed they were ever made. Besides benches, we have nothing of wood except the octagonal pedestal of the now-missing sundial. We see it in the drawing of 1859 but not that of 1850. We can therefore date it with some accuracy. It was repaired by David Cooper in 1975. I ask myself if it may not have started life as a poor box, so similar is it in design to the one that survives in Bath Abbey. Its base is a millstone, a metre in diameter. By happy chance, if chance it be, it is juxtaposed by the grave of Charles Peerless, a wheelwright whose forge stood opposite the Black Horse. He died in 1865 at the age of forty-seven.

As an immortalizer of memory, our local stone may seem little better than wood. Nor has Time been without a helping hand in its destruction: the parish magazine for February, 1974, announces, 'Several years ago a number of footstones were taken up in the churchyard so as to ease the task of maintenance, also a few illegible headstones. They were stacked at the west end of the churchyard where they have become something of an eyesore. Most of them were originally erected on graves dug at least seventy years ago, so that it is doubtful whether the people who erected them can still be consulted on their wishes. We are now advised, however, that the best thing to do is to dispose of them – they would make a handsome path or pavement – and apply the proceeds to the care of the churchyard.'

> Where we are huddled none can trace,
> And if our names remain,
> They pave some path or porch or place
> Where we have never lain!

Some of the footstones ended up on the path that leads to the back yard of the Vicarage.

The Vicarage has Elizabethan cellars, but it was rebuilt in the first half of the eighteenth century and greatly altered during the reign of Edward VII. For the best view of it, climb Amberley Mount, turn left along the South Downs Way and look back. From here its pebble-dashed gable will look like an ancient but hitherto unnoticed part of the church, one more southern thrust. You will be cozened at any hour, but most delightfully in summer before breakfast, when the sun is shining on the east walls but the south ones are in shadow. (I have not yet learnt to say 'Old Vicarage': in 2004 the incumbent moved to a new house in School Road.)

If Amberley had suffered a tsunami between the early twelfth and early sixteenth centuries, the castle and the church would have survived. As for the vicarage, it would have had little in common with the present one except the site: it was probably a mere hovel, one storey and a loft, timber-framed, walled with woven osiers that were plastered with mud, and roofed with thatch or earth. The peasants had little cause to envy their parson: he would only have been substantially richer if he had had no family to keep, but that is a big 'if': Henry I decided to exact fines from married priests, but Bishop Luffa retaliated by closing every church of his diocese. In Sussex, as the saying goes, 'We won't be druv.'

The churchyard is narrowest on the ill-favoured north and west sides, where few people have ever chosen to be buried. Like the church itself, it has always spread to the south, which is a good side, and here we come upon the oldest grave-markers. And the newest. But while the former are closest, the latter are farthest. Your best bet, of course, is to lie inside the church, but few have ever managed to afford that. Next best is to be near, within reach of the services' saving grace, not to mention that of the Reserved Sacrament. There is, however, another factor which needs to be taken into account: a grave that flanks the path, where the souls of the departed are bound to attract most prayers from passers-by, is preferable to one that does not, even if nearer to the church.

The war memorial is so situated. Rather far from the church, it is very close to the gates, which, practically speaking, have become the sole point of entry. Of Cornish granite, it is greener in its present state than the greenstone of the chancel's east end – and darker. A simple Celtic cross, it provides artists with the perfect foreground incident; and as they tend to sit, rather than stand, it towers above the church in watercolour after watercolour. It was designed in 1919 by G. Maile & son, of Euston Road, London, following a skirmish between the vicar, the Reverend Herbert Rickard, and the diocesan registrar, Ashley Tyacke, who wrote on September 15th that it 'is of a purely commercial type and the advice of the Architect should be asked before anything is erected . . . I think Mr Downing should be consulted . . . and I will delay the decree of Faculty until I hear what the Petitioners decide.' Two days later Rickard sent this riposte: ' . . . I shall ask, with all respect, that a fuller explanation of what is meant by the design being "commercial" be given . . . There has been universal approval and that not by labourers only but by a number of persons of position, culture and intelligence. You say that the advice of the Architect should be asked. I presume this means Mr H.P.B. Downing, the Diocesan Architect. It may be well to state the whole circumstances. I asked Mr Downing to give me some idea of the relative cost of a cross and a window, supposing that I was merely asking advice from the Diocesan Architect. Mr Downing took this to mean that he was to be employed for the purpose and sent me designs. The design for the Cross no one here liked, and the cost was hopelessly beyond us. I then wrote to Messrs. Maile, who submitted the design suggested – at very little more than half the cost of the other, and a very much better and more suitable design in the opinion of everyone, without exception, who saw it. When I informed Mr Downing that we were going elsewhere for the Cross, he demanded the fee of Ten Guineas for his advice. This was paid him.

'It is therefore natural enough that sitting on the Advisory Committee he should depreciate this design. But he can say nothing worse against it than that it is of a "purely commercial type".'

As long as the word 'commercial' is used pejoratively, we may rest assured that there is life left in that old dog, the Arts and Crafts Movement.

Near the foot of the shaft is inscribed the succinct

LAUS

DEO

which fits the narrow space, whereas 'Praise be to God' would have meant a squeeze. And on the rough-hewn base there follows:

THIS CROSS

WAS SET UP BY THE PEOPLE OF

AMBERLEY & HOUGHTON

AS A THANKFUL MEMORIAL BEFORE ALMIGHTY GOD

OF THE VICTORIOUS ISSUE OF THE

GREAT WAR 1914–1918

AND

OF THE DEVOTION

OF THOSE WHO FOUGHT & THOSE WHO FELL

FOR THEIR COUNTRY & FOR RIGHT

All this lettering is in inlaid lead.

Below, in front, is a separate block – not granite but ephemeral limestone – from which the inscription, carved but not inlaid, will soon have disappeared:

Amberley Church

AND

IN MEMORY OF THOSE
WHO FELL IN THE WAR
1939–45

O ye warriors of my infancy, whom I still see young, how grudgingly laconic this inscription is, not to say terse! What feeling does it prompt? Only the sure and certain hope that it will soon be illegible. Silence were a worthier tribute.

> But you shall shine more bright in these contents
> Than unswept stone, besmear'd with sluttish time.

On a sunny morning the nearby taxodium distichum casts a shadow over both wars, so that they contrast all the more tellingly with the light stone of the east end. 'Swamp cypress' is the English name, which explains why its top turns brown in times of drought. It is an American, its natural habitat stretching from Delaware to Florida, and was given by Geraldine Bethune in memory of her uncle, Lieutenant-Colonel H. S. Flower (1904–80), who commanded the 9th Battalion of the Royal Northumberland Fusiliers during the Second World War. More particularly it is an expression of esteem for his courage while a prisoner of the Japanese, 1942–45, and for the succour he gave his men. He lived at Courtyard Cottage from 1967 till his death and is buried in the churchyard of SS Cosmas and Damian, Keymer. His daughter is Sibylla Jane Flower, the historian.

*　　*　　*

Beside the porch is an altar tomb where lie interred the remains of John Harwood, a lessee of Amberley Castle. Its sides, like those of the pulpit which his descendants donated, lean outwards. The inscription runs to five lines, no two of which are in the same lettering – a typical Victorian potpourri. Around it are stumps of railings that were removed in 1939 for the war effort.

*   *   *

The cherry tree to the east of the chancel replaces a previous one and was planted in memory of Duncan Guthrie (1911–94). Close by is his tablet: set upright, scarcely clearing the grass, it is a circular slab of slate. Slate is not a local material, but the stone to which it has been affixed comes from Fittleworth, as does much of the church walls. It was made by Gary Boxall of Artists in Stone. Duncan founded and directed the charity that is now known as Action Medical Research.

It is thanks to his aunt, Elsa Noele Dalglish, that the Guthries came to live here. Wildhanger was built for them.

*   *   *

I shall now select a few of the grave-markers along the churchyard's eastern boundary:

1   The Pepper family, who owned the chalk pits, now the Amberley Working Museum, have a double headstone with carving in relief that replicates, except for the bottommost part, a late eighteenth-century one which faces the vicarage. The inscriptions occupy twin oval reserves, each surmounted by a winged cherub's head. Between them is an urn. In the angle of the chancel and the porch there another of this period, and of the same design, except that there is an urn over each oval and a winged cherub's head in the middle.

2   Edward Stott, ARA, is commemorated not only by the stained-glass window in the church but also by the tall monument that marks his grave. The inscription reads:

Amberley Church

EDWARD STOTT ARA
BORN APRIL 25 1855
DIED MARCH 19 1918
LIVED IN THIS PARISH
30 YEARS
✝ BY HIS WORKS ✝
YE SHALL KNOW HIM'

It stands halfway down the east side, and, like his *Entombment*, is indebted to the Italian sixteenth century. Flanked by two Corinthian columns, it rises to a broken pediment at whose centre is a bust of the artist,

> in whose tie
> I see a wild civility.

Tied in a bow, it careers to the south, like the church itself. And his head inclines in the same direction. His features and personality have been perfectly caught by the sculptor, his friend Francis Derwent Wood, RA, who used to stay at Vine House when it was a beerhouse called The Golden Fleece. His too is the roundel near the base. It renders Stott's last painting, *Orion*, in relief. This Boeotian hunter plucks the lyre. He is playing, I have no doubt, John Ireland's *Amberley Wild-Brooks*, a piano piece which achieves the wellnigh impossible feat of being as beautiful as its title. In *English Villages* (1975) John Burke calls it 'a tribute to the twisting and flooding waterways around one of the most captivating villages on our route.'

3   Further on lies Stott's friend and fellow-artist Francis Derwent Wood, RA, whose father was American. His monument is by Sir Edwin Lutyens, Bt., FRIBA. Simpler than the Stott monument, it is nonetheless sufficiently suggestive of the Italian High Renaissance to form a suitable frame to its chief feature, a bronze relief by Derwent

Wood himself. The subject of this, as in the Stott Window, is *The Entombment*, but here we look in vain for any sign of Amberley rustics: two naked putti, standing in prayer, flank the dead Christ, also naked, whose head rests in His mother's lap. Over them are words from the creed:

PASSVS ET

SEPVLTVS EST.

A superstructure, quite simple, with a slightly pointed pedimental head, contains the inscription:

FRANCIS DERWENT WOOD R.A.

SCULPTOR

1871 ✠ 1926

FLORENCE DERWENT WOOD

1873 ✠ 1969.

On either side, surmounting the corners, were originally two further works by Wood, seated bronze figures of Painting and Sculpture. In the 1980s they were forcibly removed: broken stone bases serve as a reminder of what we have lost. They were smaller versions of the figures which, together with Architecture and Music, adorn the Glasgow Art Gallery. In all likelihood they were cast from *maquettes* that had been submitted to the committee for approval.

4   Between these two monuments, appropriately enough, are four headstones to members of an American family whose head was Alfred Parrish (1848–1921). Hailing from Philadephia, he was an engineer, inventor and amateur artist, who came to live in Amberley, the chief attraction being Stott. He built Amberley House in 1911. The following year he gave the churchyard the two central yew trees; also

two dozen ivy plants that are happy to hide the gravemarkers when they would be better employed growing up the far end of the west wall, which is of artificial stone.

*　　*　　*

In front of the Derwent Wood monument is the grave of Elsa Noele Dalglish. She was the painter who objected to the St Edith Window. But she has better claims to fame: in her youth she was a suffragette and briefly imprisoned. In the 1930s she built good quality houses in Turnpike Road, letting them at a rent that villagers could afford. She called them End Cottages, 'END' being her initials. She died in 1948.

Somewhat further west, in line with the American graves, is a headstone by John Skelton, MBE, PRBS (1923–99). It marks the remains of Lieutenant-Colonel Theodore Doll (1916–66) who lived at Granny Read's. Words and image, which in our murals are separated – separated by centuries – are here combined: the inscription tells us that Doll was a gunner, and a relief carving of wig, quill and scroll that he was a barrister: he was called to the bar at Lincoln's Inn in June, 1948.

Near the southern end of the west wall is a headstone to Peter Bassett (1922–2000) by John Skelton's daughter, Helen Mary. It is slate, from Delabole, which seems appropriate as 'Bassett' is a Cornish name, and June, Peter's widow, is of Cornish birth. Included are notes from *An die Musik*, by Franz Schubert, but not the words they accompany, which are: '*Du holde Kunst, in wie* [*viel grauen Stunden*].' Helen Mary was asked to use italic lettering along the lines of, though not identical with, that on the oval wall-tablet to Arthur Rackham (1867–1939), the illustrator, and his wife Edyth (1867–1941), a portrait painter. They lived at Houghton House from 1920 to 1930.

*　　*　　*

To the right of the north-south path there is a Garden of Remembrance for the cremated that dates from 1961. Beyond it are five of our eleven Calvary crosses, the largest of which, with a wreath round it, all in stone, marks the grave of Walter Ruff, who died in 1901 at the age of twenty-five. His name appears on the front of the three - step plinth. Those of his father, Michael (1837–1910), and mother, Emily (1836–1911), make do with the sides, as if they were only half-persons for the loss of the son of their middle age.

Also to the right of the north-south path, but near the end, are twin headstones. The one on the right is for Simon Elwes, RA, the society portrait-painter, and his wife, Gloria, known as Golly, sister of Lady Emmet. They lived at Old Place. The inscription reads:

SIMON EDMUND VINCENT
PAUL ELWES
KNIGHT OF MALTA
ROYAL ACADEMICIAN
BORN 29TH JUNE 1902
DIED 6TH AUGUST 1975
AND HIS WIFE
GLORIA ELINOR ELWES
BORN 31ST DECEMBER 1901
DIED 8TH OCTOBER 1976
REQUIESCAT IN PACE.

Golly died in 1975, not 1976. Above, in relief carving, is Simon's shield, uncoloured, so for clarity's sake I add that it is:

or, a sesse azure, surmounted by a bend gules.

From it there protrude the eight points of the Maltese cross, an entitlement of Knights of Obedience, but not of the unfortunate Simon, who was a mere Knight of Honour and Devotion. Their son

Dominic's headstone on the left is heraldically identical, but with even less justification, for he was not a Knight of Malta at all.

The year 1975 saw the deaths of Simon on June 6th, Dominic on September 9th and Golly on October 7th. Dominic committed suicide. His mother was never told.

*   *   *

To the west of the Elwes graves is a lancet-shaped headstone to Jeremy Maas (1928–1997), 'author, art dealer and historian', who will be remembered for his salient part in the Victorian revival. The gallery that he founded in 1959 has been run since 1993 by his son Rupert.

*   *   *

A notice by the gates to the churchyard tells us:

> THESE GATES WERE CONSTRUCTED AND
> ERECTED TO COMMEMORATE THE SECOND
> MILLENNIUM AND WERE DEDICATED BY THE
> RIGHT REVEREND LINDSAY G. URWIN O.G.S.
> BISHOP OF HORSHAM ON 28TH JANUARY 2001.

These gates replace those erected in 1922, and are based on a previous design *c.*1864. The reinstated original Victorian iron arch carries a replica lantern also of Victorian design.